A *Spirited Escape*

Wilderness Empathy Teaches Response To Sociopath Vendetta

Barbara Mary Johnson

Plain View Press
P. O. 42255
Austin, TX 78704

plainviewpress.net
sb@plainviewpress.net
1-512-441-2452

Cover photo by French photographer and publisher, Danial Masse, *Spider Gap, www.livres-montagne.com.*

Acknowledgments

Helping plan glacier climb: Rangers Vladimir Stebina and Ken Dull, and Tom Borland at Seattle REI store. Ecstatic about our route, Tom gave me assurance, and what socks to buy. My children who hiked with me: Judy, Nancy, Matt; grandchildren Lauren and Nathan. Husband Ted, whose tender heels could not do a 20-mile hike, shepherded our suitcases on his five-hour boat trip. At Holden Village, Director Dianne Shiner, gardening buddy Nancy A. Johnson, her husband, carpenter Marve Johnson, teacher Cynthia LaPeta, Professor Tom Rossing (former class mate of Ted's at Luther College), guests, fellow workers, musicians, artists, people in the sauna, dining hall, bookstore all enriched my story. When I started writing, I read for groups who critiqued: Cambria Writers' Group, Nightwriters, High Hopes, and even friends in my yoga class: Kathleen Aragon, Deb Dight, and Ken Lidoff who read finished manuscript and showed me ways to improve it.

Contents

Part One: The Vendetta

Chapter One
What's Going On?

This being human is a guesthouse. Every morning a new arrival.
Rumi

"I'm taking him in." The woman deputy spoke in a monotone that cut through my law-abiding, middle-class delusions straight to despair.

"Wait till I call our lawyer." Into the house, on the phone, I cried, "This is an emergency."

With disbelief, I saw through the window my husband (for 49-plus years) in the backseat of that woman's police car. Ted wore his rolled-brim straw hat, the one he used when he whacked weeds. He was handcuffed. The receiver trembled in my hands.

The woman deputy backed up her squad car, turned around. In my imagination, I threw myself out the window in front of her official San Luis Obispo County vehicle.

Instead, I spoke on the phone to Jeff, legal counsel in our three-year harassment suit against these neighbors: "They're taking him away."

"Where are they taking him?"

"I don't know," I wailed.

The second deputy stood by the front door and shouted, "County Jail."

How could this unreal thing happen? While I was on the phone! I talked to the wall. Couldn't I chain myself to my husband, shackle him to our house, or our dog? Why didn't they see this as a grievous mistake, that the man arrested was 73 years old, and we were nice people?

Ted's relatives had called him "Professor" when he was a boy. He became an A-student in nuclear physics, an engineer in the space program, president of our church council. What had changed? The world? Or us? A new perspective had faced us when the neighbors made it clear: *We will harass you till you die.*

Jeff had said he would have a bondsperson call me. I had seen their ads and wondered what bonds had to do with jails. Now I would find out. But what will this do to our lives? Outside again, sobbing out of control, I put my head down on the hood of the remaining black-and-white car. I had never cried in front of strangers before.

"Is there anything I can do to help?" the Sergeant asked me.

Standing up, I stared at the deputy. Only the obvious came to mind–bring my husband back, rescued, protected, vindicated. What did this cop expect me to say? It was June 28, more than three years since these neighbors began tampering with our lives, one month till the Golden Wedding trip that Ted and I had planned for many years – fifty of them. At one week before the Fourth of July, a question surfaced from my deepest subconscious. "Is this still America?"

"Yes," the deputy answered. His response took me from hope to hopelessness.

Jeff had said to stay close to the phone. Our Lab, Jack-Tar, went inside the house with me, both with heads hanging low. Nothing like this had ever happened before, to our family or anyone we knew. This event etched itself on my violated self, like something in a mystery thriller.

My mind whirled with pictures of jail, superimposed on a sentimental golden anniversary greeting card. I stared at the kitchen sink. Ted and I had become puppets with no control of our lives. The neighbors, the sheriff's department, and whatever they believed about us determined our fate. This line-up of events had become "a crowd of sorrows," as cited by 13th century poet Rumi, "who violently sweep your house empty of its furniture..."

Within sight of the phone, I sat at the dining room table, moved to the window seat, walked through the kitchen, bedroom, and back again. In our fifty years together, Ted and I had argued and worried about trivial things compared to this accusation of assault. Quite recently Ted had disagreed with my suggested golden wedding plans: "If I had my druthers, we'd just go out to dinner for our anniversary. Have some champagne."

Plans seemed unimportant now. Yet after a torrent of pros and cons, we had agreed to be volunteer workers for a month at Holden Village. A remote retreat owned by the Lutheran church in north-central Washington's Glacier Peak Wilderness, it was accessible only by boat or back-packing. I wanted to hike in, which included climbing Spider Gap Glacier. Our three grown children and two grandchildren agreed to go with me. Because of heel problems, Ted couldn't hike but would take the boat. Now he might have to appear at a courtroom trial and we would have to learn how to prepare for such a thing.

Ripped from my husband's side, I waited for the bondswoman's call. Bailing out a mate-of-50-years belongs in some detective novel, not in our life. I had no idea how the system worked, knew nothing about arrests, bookings, jails, arraignments, hearings, and trials. I didn't read police stories or watch cop shows on TV. With faith, fury and frenzy, I steeled myself to do anything to save Ted.

The phone rang. It was a bondswoman named Rosemary: "Your husband's bail is $20,000. It's a criminal charge. You pay me 10 percent. How do you want to handle that?"

I gave her our credit card number. She repeated numbers and expiration date just like a catalog clerk. She told me where the jail was. "I'll wait for you in the lobby to sign the papers. How long will it take you to get there?"

"Thirty minutes." Throwing on clean jeans and a cotton shirt, not knowing if appropriate or not, I wondered if my clothes could affect his case. Jack-Tar rode in the backseat as my Jeep crept out our winding dirt road, through rolling pastures back dropped by coastal mountains, and past our irrational, sociopath neighbor. He stood on the shared easement and laughed hysterically. One of the lawyers in the harassment suit had called him and his wife "evil people whose house should burn down, with them inside of it." But I knew that the poet Rumi had written: "...treat each guest honorably...(they) may be clearing you out for some new delight." I found that hard to believe.

After Rosemary, a serious business-woman, gathered the signed bail papers, she warned me that Ted might not be released immediately.

"You mean like 15, 20 minutes?" I asked.

"More like an hour." She pointed to the door where he would appear.

Part of the turbulent County Jail lobby, I sat on a bus-terminal-type bench. The metal door periodically slid open to reveal a released person. Ted would be able to see me as soon as he stepped out.

Since it was Friday, many "weekend" prisoners reported in the lobby for duty. They formed a line and chatted.

"Do you have a pen?" a man asked me. Shaking my head, even though my purse carried extras, I couldn't participate in this community. That metal door held my attention.

"How about a pencil?"

"Sorry."

This was unlike me, but I shunned human contact after the laughing neighbor, parade of deputies, lawyer on the phone, and Rosemary here at the jail. I couldn't respond to the man in need of a pencil. The air drooped with staleness.

"The dark thought, the shame, the malice," writes Rumi, "you meet them at the door, laughing and invite them in." I had no energy for such entertaining, and felt scarred for life.

I stepped outside to console Jack-Tar, stuck in the parking lot, and walked him around before resuming my lonely job of bailer. For the first hour, the turmoil in the lobby held me spellbound. One released man only wore bright blue boxer shorts. On the lobby phone, he explained how he had no clothes and needed a ride home. Another free man, fully dressed, stepped into a waiting cab.

I waited for my husband. Frigid air-conditioning chilled the metal furniture, walls, floor and bullet-proof windows that separated us from the clerks. Deputies arrived with casseroles of food; they must have been having a potluck for the Friday-night shift. Garlic, oniony aromas tantalized me. It was 6:00 PM, an hour and a half since my arrival.

Rosemary had told me there would be a hearing in two weeks. She seemed optimistic but that might be part of her operative mode. She had said earlier on the phone that Ted would only be charged with a misdemeanor and released on his own recognizance. She was wrong. Neither of those things had happened, and his trial might be on August 16, our anniversary date.

A sinister door had slammed on me, hit me in the back, pinched my fingers. I pleaded my case, in my head, in front of some television-type judge, and argued with logic and examples from our lives. But I suspected that no one listened.

Poet Rumi had an answer: "Be grateful for whoever comes, because each had been sent as a guide from beyond." What kind of guide; and where is this *beyond*?

The County Jail clock reached 7:15 PM. I feared how Ted might be treated here in jail, as the hours slouched by. Might I have to sleep on this bench that was designed with dividers so no one could? I walked up to the thick glass, with its circular metal talk-through device like a movie box-office. "Is there some problem?"

"These things take awhile," the young woman said.

"But we paid the bail two hours ago. He's 73 years old and he hasn't had dinner."

"He will be out soon," she said.

Apparently, everyone else had been taken care of, and that sliding door opened no more. I returned to my bench in the empty lobby and another 30 minutes went by. I addressed the bulletproof glass again. "Can't something be done? Keeping him here this long is cruel and unusual punishment. He's wrongly accused."

"He's been given a blanket," the young woman told me. "He's sleeping."

"Sleeping?" I sat down and pictured him in a cell, on a cot and returned to her window. My knees weakened. "May I have a blanket, too? I'm very cold."

"Oh, no, we can't do that."

"Is there someone else I can talk to?"

Her supervisor appeared. "It's the computer breakdown that is delaying your husband's release. We can't give him a case number until –"

"We can call for the number. We only live a half hour from here. We can drive back to get the number. Don't you trust us for that? You've got the $20,000. Why can't he go home?"

Some of the deputies in the next room looked up at me, disrupting their potluck. If they had invited me, they could have heard my story. The supervisor kept her tone cordial, insisting nothing could be done. I used the lobby phone to leave a woeful message for our lawyer. and returned to my cold bench to fret. Thomas Merton had written that we are "consoled and strengthened by being hopeless."

My mind surveyed recent and long-gone conversations on "love my neighbor as myself" and "turn the other cheek." This ultimate challenge tested me with a true-life situation. How could we love unlovable neighbors? I didn't see how we could forgive this travesty. Ted had been arrested, not knowing why the deputies believed the neighbor's story, without a chance to plead his innocence. No matter how things turned out, Ted would have a criminal record as a felon. How could we not fight back?

Such words, *felon* and *criminal record*, stalled my consciousness in disbelief. It wasn't fair. We had done nothing wrong. We were innocent victims. The door slid open and I sobbed out loud.

There was Ted in his weed-whacking hat, free of handcuffs. He looked amazed and relieved, smaller, skinnier and more delicate than before. Definitely older, more pale and vulnerable. My throat tightened and eyes blurred. I wondered how many more years together did we have? I snatched him to me and took him home for a late dinner. We drove across our shared easement; the neighbor was nowhere to be seen.

Ted could hardly eat our simple supper. He pushed his soup bowl back and put down the crusty piece of sourdough: "I think I'll just go to bed."

While he showered I took the spread off and crawled into my side of the platform bed he had built for us half a century before. Ted shuffled toward his side of the bed. "I'm so tired."

I held him in my arms like a child with a nightmare. "Everything's going to be all right."

"We'll get over this," he mumbled.

I kept contact with him all night with my arm, leg, foot or forehead. A heart-rending sigh of forlornness escaped from my sleeping husband. My mind-screen viewed all that I knew about our neighbors. I saw them as guides from beyond the inferno: a gnome and witch.

Self Love

I spoon creme brulée past my lips
to palette and tongue
crunch my teeth on crispy toast
spread with apricot jam
suck in morning breeze
till lungs share it
with every cell from
cowlick to baby toes.

I listen to my spirit
and love myself.

Can I turn
my cheek
to love a neighbor
this much?

barbara marysdaughter

Chapter Two

Hazards At Home

> *Only myth, only narrative can capture the mystery of*
> *human goodness and evil...*
> Paul Baumann, Editor of *Commonweal*

My night spirit wings down to mythical, bombastic discords. The nightmare in my head becomes a battleground torment of music from Handel's *Messiah*. *Why do the nations so furiously rage together; why do the people imagine a vain thing?* Chords and minor keys pull me into a black dream where the gnome and witch live under a little bridge.

In my hopeless fantasy, this crude wooden bridge resembles the one that crosses the creek on our shared easement. Ted once dreamed of driving his bulldozer across that bridge to stop the gnome from blocking our roadway.

Through the mist I see Ted and me drive a chariot across that bridge. The gnome shakes his fist, delivers curse after curse after curse upon us. He is huge and loud: "I will make your life miserable."

To escape, we drive across the bridge, up the dirt road in our Fury Fantasy Chariot, again and again and again. We need to run errands, try to get the mail and go to the hardware store but cannot.

A phantom parade-float crowds the side of the easement that is on our property. Something is piled on top of the float. We hope it's food, candy, flowers, wrapped packages for us. Perhaps there is another troll, one with gifts for us.

Our chariot navigates its repetitive journey with fast turn-arounds, though the vehicle has no engine and no horses to pull it. Winds and whirlpools of mist move us onward, turn us at our gate to go back through dark woods, over the bridge, past the cursing Billygoat gruff gnome. Computerized calendars record the length of this harassment-go-around at three years, or one thousand days.

The chariot stops, dumps us into a muddy manure pile. In its fumes, Ted and I sniff out the truth. The imagined float is a flat-bed trailer loaded with auto-parts, engine bits, plastic rubbish, barbed wire and broken mirrors. Iron stakes block the roadway. Can bulldozers, at full throttle, demolish nightmares and push us through this Slough of Despair?

We can not see our gate. Safety is beyond reach. We want to hide in our dream house, the home planned for four decades that Ted designed for our golden years.

We're vulnerable, twenty-to-thirty years older than gnome and witch, who have cut us off from our longed-for, remaining years of life. Gunshot rings out, followed by hysterical giggling. Two mules thunder down the hill toward us. We leave the chariot to search for paths through the woods but locked gates turn us away. Skidding down the muddy bank of the creek, we stumble on its rocky streambed. A flash flood sweeps us to the edge. Overhanging branches whip us like the tree limbs that harassed Snow White. A large tree falls to block our path. Cries of birds taunt us by sounding like the Wicked Witch:

"You ran over our dog."

"You poisoned our mule."

Lies, lies, I scream before judges in the highest court, but they don't hear me. To get even by using the truth is a vain thing. Ted's bulldozer, on automatic programming, demolishes the gnome's workshop – where the gnome makes knives and guns.

The creek bends. We try to climb its bank. A good life awaits us if we can reach our home. Heavy fog drifts in. Apparitions moan:

"You steal tools from our shed."

"Your surveys are wrong."

"You lie."

"None of these things are true," I shout out.

Sinkholes suck off shoes. We slip on steep, greasy clay. Eyes of the lynx glisten at edge of the woods. Poison oak brushes our faces, hands. The earth trembles and spits out a flow of lava. Beethoven's Ninth, St. James Infirmary Blues, Pachelbel's Canon goad us on. We plough through all obstacles, surge past. We are part of Pilgrim's Progress, while threats grow louder in our ears.

"We are your enemies for life."

"We will harass you till you die."

Ted and I grasp at roots, leap up the incline, make little switchbacks out of steep topography. We hear the vendetta.

"...and then we will harass your grandchildren's grandchildren."

These encounters with the gnome and witch whip us with stress, worries, insomnia, nightmares, sinus infections, allergies, mucus, ear infections, doctors' appointments, tests, hearing aids, bills. We write pages of good thoughts, speak peaceful ideas, sing friendly messages, pray for help. Hold back desires for *a burning bridge, auto accident, incurable diseases. Keep diaries and records, take pictures, write letters, change lawyers, pay their bills.*

Curses transpose into discordant dirges played on a gloomy organ by hands in boxing gloves. An old toilet, decorated with mud or worse, stands in our path. We step around to see the phantom float dump its cargo by our gate and look up through oak leaves at a night sky of familiar stars. They lead us home to safety.

But the torture goes on. Insurance companies appoint lawyers, arbitrators, mediators (why not meditators?). Judges, court deputies, courthouse employees foster fears, stifle lives, tell us not to expect fairness "for everyone lies under oath nowadays." We listen to more lies, pay bills, and grasp at agencies, county services, state offices, elder-abuse experts, victim/witness groups. Fish and game people check fragile headwaters of our creek for polluting manure, to no avail. We give up, but know we cannot. We ponder Thomas Merton's advice: "... in the end, it is reality of personal relationship that saves everything."

The next morning messages from our two daughters filled the computer screen in our extra room. I had emailed them the dreadful news while waiting for the bondswoman's call. Our son, with no computer, learned from his answering machine that his father had been arrested.

When Matt called back, his father talked about the easement road and what had happened. "I can't believe it," Matt exploded. "The police didn't believe my father? They thought the crazy neighbor was telling the truth?"

Ted tried to explain the inexplicable. Matt promised to keep in touch. "I love you, Dad."

The old oak trees just outside the windows bounced and swayed their branches. Together in our sunny, cheerful guest/computer room, Ted and I read the reply from Judy. Our eldest child admonished her father to never again talk with or even look at that neighbor. "That's the only way to handle someone like him. Pretend he doesn't exist."

Nancy, two years younger than her sister and living in Oregon, had telephoned the arresting deputy in San Luis Obispo to object to the wrongful arrest of her father. The Sergeant, the one who had assured me this was still America, told her that since the neighbor had made the initial complaint, "we tend to believe the charge that the first caller makes."

What? Why had it taken us three years of harassment – conferring with lawyers, deputies, and even a 30-minute phone conversation with the sheriff – to learn this basic fact?

On the phone, Ted told Nancy how earlier, the neighbor had placed a stake on our side of the easement as a challenge. "I had removed that wooden stake," Ted continued, " when the Gnome appeared and took it. He tried to hit me with it. He's made threatening moves like that before. I never thought of calling the sheriff...to make that crucial 'first call.'"

Jeff, our lawyer, phoned to tell us that Ted's hearing would be in August and warned Ted, "You must be in that courtroom or forfeit your $20,000 bond."

The arraignment came first, in two weeks. At 8:15 a.m., we met Jeff at his office, walked across the street to the courthouse, checked the list of criminal cases. Ted's name wasn't there.

Jeff settled us in the cafeteria while he called the District Attorney's office. Amid the aroma of coffee and sweet rolls, we imagined outlandish things that might happen: Ted in prison clothes and chains, rats crawling on his cot, our house burned down, dog slaughtered. Our memories fed upon courtroom movies, accounts of prison riots, and our own nightmares.

Our lawyer approached at a good clip, his right hand out, a big smile on his face: "Ted, you're a free man. The D.A. dropped the charges. There is no case."

When asked why the charges were dropped, Jeff shrugged and mumbled something about the slow wheels of justice.

Ted and I would escape to the wilderness with our family after all. The two of us could work in the wilderness-village for a month, enjoy its concerts, discussion groups, art classes, vespers, and sauna where the towels carried the message: Holy Hot Hilarity. We needed that mirth-filled theology more than ever. Yet these troubles rattled around my brain. Ted's name, on the criminal record of felons, still remained there. We knew the harassment would also continue.

Revenge duked it out with forgiveness. Did all these visiting ideas clear us out for some new delight? Will it be the wilderness?

Neighborly Questions

Are all members
of the human race
our neighbors
to be loved as ourselves?

What about dogs and horses?
shall we include bacteria
inside and outside our bodies
as beloved as ourselves?

How about stones trees oceans
and stars to be loved?

Does our planet love the sun
can earth moon over the moon?
Is it attracted
to the star Scorpio
or red planet Mars?

Do our arms adore our shoulders?
And do little toes
care about our nose?

Is every human our neighbor?
Can we love each one
as we love ourselves?
Could we love human terrorists
who plan our destruction?

How can
we know
such love?

barbara marysdaughter

Part Two: The Glacier Climb

Chapter Three
Who Will Hear Us When We Fall?

Phelps Creek Trailhead 2400'
7 mi. to Spider Meadow 5300'

Judy showed us the battered ice ax, with folding blade and stout handle, that she had rented for $20. "They sell for ninety," our daughter added, as we headed for our take-off spot. "I thought we might need it to make toe-holds in the snow or...well, you never know."

Two hours riding on this lonely road through the forest to Phelps Creek Trailhead allowed us to confirm this edge on our hiking trip – it's unsure, hey-we're-not-mountaineers cast. My family had not trained for this adventure. Busy schedules interfered with their learning how to use an ice ax, breaking in new boots and racking up miles hiked. Because of heel problems, Ted would duck out with passage on the Lady of the Lake steamer, the only other way to get to Holden Village. All of us carried with us the wrongful-arrest episode and the shadow of what might come next when Grandpa and Grandma went home.

Determined to hike in, I had completed six months of trainer hikes with the Sierra Club, and sought detailed advice from rangers, and from Tom, a Seattle REI (Recreation Equipment Inc.) clerk. He had recently hiked our route through Spider Meadow, gone over the Gap and slid down into Lyman valley. His experience helped me rise to my Queen Bee position as exalted exposition leader.

On our fifty-mile drive to the trailhead, my right-leg calf-muscle tensed and foot cramped. With laces hastily undone, I ripped off my boot to massage my aching foot and leg.

"You Ok, Grandma?" asked my granddaughter Lauren, a tough, blonde, blue-eyed soccer-player at eighteen years old.

"Just thinking about the hike, hoping everyone likes Holden Village when we get there." I smiled at my firstborn grandchild. "Thinking about everything, including bears." Steve Heraro's book, *Bear Attacks*, had alerted me to black bears, the kind in Glacier Peak Wilderness "that usually attack during the day." The author describes a woman field-geologist who lost both arms to a bear attack. Another rapacious bear left "a length of intestine, eight feet long, hanging from a tree branch" near the body of a dead child.

"We have to stay within sight of each other on the trail," I advised, "and everything should be a group decision." This ride in Matt's van gave me a chance to instruct my crew but I wasn't sure they heard me.

Ted addressed our family group next. "You know, I want to walk with you for an hour or so. Then I'll hang around the parking lot, in case you have to turn back."

Ouch. That remark smarted like we'd been hit with the ice ax. If our team can't make it, can't climb up or around Spider Glacier, can't get over Spider Gap to the Lyman Lakes, there's no alternative except hiking back to the trailhead. With no vehicle there, we would have to hitch a ride to the boat dock 100 miles away.

Ted's plan to wait there on Day One of this three-day hike might swing the group to skip the glacier. We could chicken out and take the Lake Chelan boat with Grandpa. Would that be a relief or disappointment?

I looked at our driver Matt, a hefty guy, determined and competitive mountain biker as well as motorcycle racer. In his teens, Matt had never expected to live beyond the age of 25 (he had told us recently) because of wild chances he took. Was he more cautious in his 40s?

Nancy, our middle child who trained and rode her two Arabian horses, had already made it clear: "I'm not good with slippery footing." When four people recently fell into a Mt. Hood crevasse, not too far from her home in Oregon, their deaths changed her mind about our glacier climb. She opted for the boat with her Dad. Then Nancy rejoined us hikers when a ranger offered an alternate, safer route skirting the glacier.

Judy had, in her teen years, survived falling down a High Sierra waterfall, with only bruises. Her teen-aged children, Lauren and Nathan (who played trombone in the school band) remained unpredictable, unread chapters on their first backpack. Fourteen-year-old son, Tyler had stayed home with his father, explaining, "I like to bike, not hike."

At 10:00 am in the trailhead parking lot, mountain peaks soared above us. Pure mountain air expanded our lungs. I wanted to yodel us on our way, into this backpack that answered a long-time dream of mine. Away from the gnome and the witch at last, Ted and I could work out something to bring about peace with our difficult neighbors.

With belly-bands tightened, we felt our packs, from 25-to-35 pounds, sag from our shoulders. Nancy carried in her pack the bulky bear-proof food container that didn't fit in mine. We applied sun block, stuffed jackets into packs, and took final pictures with glacier-peak background.

Ted, away from our neighbor problems, glowed like an anointed pilgrim, already cleansed by the wilderness.

Nancy and I squinted at the bulletin board's faded note from hikers who had attempted the climb: "Slippery glacier–can't make it to the Gap." I held my breath over that word *slippery*, but Nancy took more pictures. She was with us, starting and not turning back. Standing tall, dedicated.

Matt locked the van and Ted pocketed the keys for his drive to the lake's boat dock. We wouldn't see him again for three days up the trail and glacier, and over that 7100-foot Gap, if all went well.

Is this any way to celebrate fifty years of marriage? Not traveling together? One of my friends had claimed, "That's what makes marriage work."

We started. Ted carried a water bottle and one old ski pole for a walking stick. Chilling fog floated between trees and over our path. Rounded boulders helped us cross six raging creeks.

"My topo map only shows four creeks to cross," I whined. "What other surprises will there be?"

Phelps Creek, most prominent on my map, had captured my attention for 18 months of planning. One of the old miners, according to guidebooks, had carried heavy equipment up the mile-long Spider Gap glacier. If he could do that, surely we could haul ourselves up, with packs filled with the barest necessities.

After maneuvering another tricky, rock-hopping creek, Ted said it was time for him to go back. He handed the ski pole to Nancy and shouted over the babble of water. "You might want this."

"But you'll need it to get back to the van," she argued.

"I'll be OK." Ted asked us if we wanted him to wait at the gate. "I could be there around five o'clock this afternoon in case you have to turn around, can't make it over the Gap."

Would we all end up on the Lake Chelan boat with Grandpa? It sounded comforting, safe. But to give up our three-day backpack would puncture my dream of the family hiking with me on this holy pilgrimage to the wilderness, the place where Ted and I would rediscover ourselves, solve the gnome-and-witch problem..

"Do you want me at the trailhead this afternoon?" Ted repeated. "What about it?"

"Naw."

"We'll be all right."

"Don't worry about us."

Our gang expressed confidence, after one-and-a-half hours of hiking. No budding blisters? Had they forgotten the sad note on the bulletin board: "Slippery glacier—can't make it to the Gap." Perhaps they remembered the encouragement from Ranger Vladimir: "Our 100-degree weather has melted that thick snow cover and you can make it without crampons and ice axes."

The majesty of these dense woods and exuberant creeks might have filled my family with promise for our climb. Did they recall the guidebook pictures I had mailed them of breathtaking mountainscapes? Were they eager to see such splendor?

After quick farewells with Ted, because we had to arrive at the campsite before dark, our hiking team turned back to the trail. I waved till I could see my husband no more. He looked as vulnerable and alone as he had when that jail door slid open.

Ted had been our family's leader 40 years previously, climbing Mt. Whitney. We should have carried his supplies on this hike so he could be with us. But in my gut, I knew he wouldn't allow us to take on his burden.

My shoulders needed to relax which is hard to do while lugging a backpack. My spine ramrodded my head into leader-like posture. Shoulder blades inched down my back, away from my ears. Everything would work out. Our family will be together in the village for two days after the hike, as part of their golden-wedding gift to us. Then Ted and I will jump into our four-week commitment of volunteer work as carpenter and gardener, starting a life apart from what we left at home.

Around the curve, workers sawed off limbs of trees to relocate a muddy trail. Inhaling the woody aroma, I asked, "Do you know if the Gap is passable today?"

A man in a checkered shirt answered, "Haven't heard a thing."

A small logjam served as a bridge at the next creek crossing. We admired the expertise of a muscular man and woman stepping quickly across. When I asked about Spider Gap, the woman spoke plaintively, "We couldn't climb the glacier yesterday because of wind and rain."

Ice axes hung from their packs; surefootedness in scarred boots spoke of experience. The man scowled. "Our car is parked at Trinity because we had planned to do a loop. Now we'll have to hitch a ride."

The woman gave us a wan smile and walked on down the path. Nathan, Nancy and I exchanged glances, since we three were ahead. "What do you think of that?" I asked.

"We'll make it OK," said Nathan who at six feet tall evoked great confidence. An hour later he asked his mother if he could hitchhike back to San Francisco. "I don't see the point of this."

Maybe the old 1986 Porsche that he bought with his earned money, called to him about needing repairs. But his mother said to keep going.

A loud crack, like a gunshot, slashed through the silence. My eyes focused on a single trunk in the densely packed forest to our right as that tree began to lean over, slowly. Nathan and Nancy watched the dream-like pageantry with me. The dying giant fell in slow motion within its silent forest. Then toppled faster. This angled tree gathered speed in its destiny to meld with the earth. We waited for the death rattle.

A ghastly thunderous thud filled the forest, echoed from the trunks of the live trees, and pressed against our ear drums. The tree dug its grave, sent out tremors that slammed through the thick soles of our boots. My feet tingled with its vibrations, and the novel idea that I shared this moment with a tree.

The dead giant didn't hit anything except its own composting floor. We saw, heard and recognized the corpse on the ground, and the hole it left in the woods. Living trees around it stood silent like we did. Why did the tree fall at this precise time? Was it a good sign for us, or a foreboding? Who will catch us when we fall?

Compared to our escape from neighbors' threats of knives at our throats, guns at our heads, what does a tree falling in the forest mean? Does its demise mean failure or the end of some phase, a new life, a change in thinking? Did Ted, back at the trailhead by now, hear the tree fall in our forest?

Rounding a corner, our trail invited us into a giant garden perfumed by wild flowers, nourished by bubbling streams, fed by waterfalls fueled by snowfields in the surrounding hanging cliffs of Red Mountain. Spider Meadow! We were there and it was stunning, like Seattle Tom of REI had told me.

Peopled with friendly, waving campers, the meadow welcomed us. One of the men, wearing hiking shorts and a large T-shirt to cover his fold-over gut, came over to greet us. He said, "Beautiful day."

Yes, the sun shone through cloud fragments in a brilliant sky, but our mind-focus was on the glacier.

"I climbed it this morning," the camper said with a big smile. "It was easy."

We gathered around him. Did he have crampons and an ice ax? What about the couple with axes who couldn't get through yesterday?

"It rained yesterday, but today is fine. I just used a hiking stick. And no pack, of course. I went up, and back down to my tent here."

Dancing a little jig, in spite of my pack, I celebrated sun, earth, the fallen tree's life, and this man who was an angel, a mountaineer unawares. If he could do it, we could, too. All six of us listened to him, asked questions, and smiled. Even Nathan, who had grouched about stubbing his toe in the motel room that morning, and had failed to see any reason to continue this hike.

Lauren's blue eyes sparkled. "Let's go."

Our informant continued, "There's a hairy creek-crossing before you climb the mountain."

"Is that Phelps Creek?" I asked.

"Yep," he said. "A raging, swollen river with a big log-jam for a bridge. If you go at it slow and easy, and take your time, you can make it."

We waved and smiled and thanked the happy fat man. In a communal burst of confidence, our group of six headed toward the mountain trail to our campsite and the foot of Spider Gap, but first, the crossing of Phelps Creek.

Enjoy Spider Meadow, I told myself. Take in the comfort. Breathe in the sweetness of the air. Delight in these mountains, richness of color and all the creeks. Look at each flower; bless it for being here. Lose yourself in this wilderness, become more than a victim of harassment. Be a trekker on your way to the "hairy" creek. Take it slow and easy.

Our trail brought us past other hikers' tents and closer to the dreaded crossing. The sun was low. Afternoon shadows stretched out on the meadow floor. Striding out with my family at a good pace, I spun into a new dimension with a positive attitude for the glacier climb, balanced against the dangers of this crossing. Harmonious chords, not unlike the Hallelujah Chorus, filled my consciousness with confidence. We would make it, and continue to do wonderful things forever and ever, and ever.

Sociopaths

The American Psychiatric Association estimates
three percent of all males in our country are
sociopath.

A list of common sociopath traits:
egocentricity, callousness, impulsivity,
conscience defect, exaggerated sexuality...

Chapter Four
Dangerous Crossing

> Spider Meadow
> Phelps Creek crossing 5300'
> To Larch Knob campsite 6400'

After we conquered that 40-foot-wide Phelps Creek which summoned us to its churning chaos, we planned to celebrate. If we made it across, we could rest and eat lunch. Grandpa wouldn't have to worry about us. Of course, there was no way to tell him that. Cell phones didn't work in this wilderness. We had no tour guide, no Sierra Club leader, but trekked under the guidance of Grandma, age 73.

Lauren, with a red bandana tied around her blond hair, strode out ahead with Nathan, both jazzed by the new challenge of the dangerous crossing. Soon enough, we heard our teenagers hoot and holler.

"Sounds like shouts of success," I said to their mother.

"Maybe, fear," Judy answered.

The creek bellowed like a dragon anticipating prey, from its cover of small trees and giant boulders. My shoulders tensed, tried to cover my ears. But I wanted to study the creek, before starting across, to see its dangers, loopholes, tricks and surprises. Judy, Nancy and I searched for an approach to the thing.

"This way," said Nancy, with her authoritative Project-Feasibility-Manager voice. On vacation from her job, she was the boss and guided us along a creek side path. We could see Matt, jaunty in his outback hat, start to balance on the mishmash of logs. He looked fearless and confident.

Matt landed safely and Lauren balanced her way back again to show us where to start. We three had had wilderness experience with water. Nancy and Judy in the High Sierra, and me in a Kern River white-water rafting over-board tumble.

A dozen tree trunks wedged into the creek banks like a pile of pick-up sticks, enormous but narrow, slippery and studded with offshoots. Many limbs lay under the water, held fast by rocks. All together, they bridged the forceful stream.

"Don't want to be on this when it comes apart," I cried out.

Incessant, tumbling water shrieked too loud to talk over, or even to think it through. None of us remembered the 75 feet of rope in my pack, to tie to trees on each side for a handrail. Nobody suggested we loosen our pack straps, an honored hiking safety move. The weight of our packs could drag us under the water if we fell in the roiling, bubbling water beneath our 40-foot logjam. Who will catch us when we fall?

"We'll put Mom in the middle," Judy shouted, flipping her blonde braid out of the way, as she tested the logs for a foothold. "I'll go first, then Mom, then Nancy." Lauren crossed for the third time to direct her mother's footsteps. My composure jilted with my first step but I reveled in my granddaughter's concern. A top-heavy backpack made me tipsy on the logs. With an old ski pole, and a broken branch, I stabilized myself. Each footstep seemed solid in spite of holes where trunks fit loosely together. The bridge looked endless and its three-foot width gave me few options. Icy water below slapped giant boulders around. With tai-chi relaxation, I lowered shoulders, collarbone, rib cage and groin area to feel balanced, grounded. But I couldn't get the hang of whatever taunted my equilibrium.

Applying philosophy to the physical, I followed Judy's choices, found her footholds to progress three-fourths of the way across. I repeated to myself. "Can't fall now" over and over and plodded along. Judy landed , with her camera ready.

"Ohhhhhhhhh."

It was Nancy, I knew, down in the icy water. All the way? Bouncing against the rocks? Helpless because of her pack? I couldn't turn or I might fall, too. Nancy's voice soared above the creek's noise, "I'm OK, all right."

"What happened?"

"A log became a see-saw."

"And I got the picture," Judy crowed.

I leapt ashore, looked back to see Nancy in water up to her knees. The current pushed her against the logjam. On the other side of the bridge, she would have been swept downstream. She had told us she "didn't like slippery footing." Words like catastrophe and disaster filled my head and stretched my muscles and bones to their limits.

Nancy bunched up her wet pants, pulled herself along with the help of the ski pole her father had given her. "I can make it."

My throat clogged and body chilled. I was close to tears over what might have happened. Hands reached out to help Nancy. We cheered and then we kidded her:

"Didn't you fall in the creek on the Whitney hike?"

Nancy unrolled her pant legs so the sun could dry them. She sat down to consider lunch. Our provisions offered mozzarella on an English muffin.

The scattered boulders we all sat upon for lunch kept their distance from each other. So did we, unintentionally. But maybe we needed some quiet time to recharge our bodies, clear out creek fears from our mind, feed the stomach, contemplate what came next. The waters still bellowed like a dragon and we made room for the next-day fears of the glacier.

Eight college-age men, without backpacks, ran over the logjam bridge like it was nothing. We watched them in disbelief. They waved and ran past us, in good spirits. They didn't seem to know that this was a hairy crossing.

"But only where there is a dangerous crossing," cautioned an article in Holden's newsletter, "can we find liberation." Another writer, Paul Loeb asks, "Am I perishing? I don't ask this question calmly. I am struggling how I might contribute to reversing this descent into fear and sorrow, to help restore hope."

Hope and liberation. That's what we needed. At Holden, controversial crossings of ideas bring generations together in liberating searches for new answers. Ted and I hoped our family would enjoy such community opportunities, and we counted on it to free ourselves from the hateful vendetta.

Our three generations had accomplished a liberating crossing here. Looking danger in the face, we persevered. The next day demanded more from us hikers, whatever it takes to climb a glacier.

Chewing slowly on my dry cheese sandwich, I shrank from the idea of crossing the creek again. This was the time and place of no return. Even Nathan hadn't mentioned going back lately.

Lauren finished her lunch and wanted to start up the trail to our tentsite, near the foot of Spider Glacier. "Let's go."

Many hairpins turned our path to gain the 6400-foot altitude of Larch Knob campground. Thirty-five years earlier, Ted had led our family up Mt. Whitney's 97 switchbacks and we gained unforgettable memories. I called out, "Remember Whitney?"

Matt groaned. "You pushed me all the way up those switchbacks."

Nancy moaned. "I fell in the creek at Mirror Lake, and had altitude sickness at the top. I also counted the switchbacks."

Spider Gap's trail switched endlessly, painfully like Whitney's. Leg muscles and blistered feet screamed but everyone kept going. This convoluted trail became our *Pilgrim's Progress* with "touches of sublimity, madness, despair and ecstasy." We climbed a slope named *Difficulty*.

Delectable Mountain surrounded us. We weren't carrying a 50-pound anvil, or was I? Memories of the arrest, jail scene, and laughing Gnome all weighted my burden, and became my anvil.

Ted had researched that first backpack. He checked topo maps, compass, and shopped for supplies. Now I wouldn't see Ted for two more days. He couldn't help me. Was he worried sick about us, and have good reason to be? He might hang out in the van, at the trailhead tonight, just in case we turned back. What will he be worrying about?

My imagined presence to his concern for us zigzag trekkers, relaxed my leg muscles, soothed my feet. Sleep should come easily in our tents on Larch Knob. My family could rest well at the toe of the Spider Glacier *courlair*, or corridor. Tomorrow we would awake ready and eager to climb.

Our day's pilgrimage ended at this tree-studded Knob, spread out from its wooded mother-mountain like an observation deck showing us the meadow 1100 feet below. Matt and Nathan pitched their tent at the extreme outer edge of the Knob. Happy to be there, we tossed our concerns down that cliff.

"We're in trouble if it rains," Matt reminded Nathan, his tent mate. "There's no rain fly." Matt, who lived in southern California, added, "It never rains in summer."

Snow-patched crags hovered above us. The toe of Spider Glacier waited within spitting distance. Most of us tired hikers rejected the chance to even look at it. More interested in our own toes and body functions, we noticed a welcome sign pointing up another trail, proclaiming "toilet".

Judy and Nancy started up the path first. When they returned, Judy proclaimed, "It's too far."

"Nothing but a wooden box in the middle of some bramble. A cruel joke." Nancy looked like she'd had enough surprises for the day. Our youngest hikers, Nathan, Lauren and Matt bounded over to check out the glacier.

After struggling against the incline to that outside outhouse, I reported back: "I'm not going to do that again."

Our younger glacier inspectors returned, ecstatic. "We can climb it."

"It will be easy."

"It's do-able and beautiful."

Confident about the glacier, triumphant over Phelps' Creek, and smug about camping in this perfect spot, we relaxed. We could have crawled into our sleeping bags right then and slept straight through till sunrise. But my children cranked up the little camp stove. Soon our freeze-dried dinners wafted sensory aromas of chicken Alfredo, tomato soup and applesauce.

We dined 100 yards from tent sites, just like the bear-attack book advised. We chowed down and watched the sun say good night. After clean-up, we happily slipped into slumber.

Around midnight, tent mates Nancy and I crept outside to empty insistent bladders. We didn't climb up to the wooden box.

Outsized stars blazed above snow patches on the peaks. Their white-ness broadcast a rare luminescence, a message that seemed to say we were cared for, held in the love of creation, with assurance for the next day's climb. We felt healing properties in the sparkling snow, like bonding with the fallen tree. I said to Nancy, "The glowing snow is promising to hear us if we fall. To catch us."

"Why didn't something catch me when I fell in the creek?" Nancy asked and added, "We won't fall any more. I've done it. For all."

Back in the tent to sleep, we heard drops falling on our tent's rain fly. Yikes! We'd forgotten to trench around the tent. That meant a wet tent-floor.

Besides that, my water bottle, with its loose cap, tipped over and soaked my sleeping bag. Without a rain-fly cover, Matt's tent would be flooded.

In the morning, it was still raining. Matt's voice floated through the early mist from his on-the-edge tent site. "You might as well get up, Nathan. It's not going to get any dryer."

Inside our tent, Nancy and I silently inspected our soggy sleeping bags. Wet! All because a bottle cap hadn't been tightened, and that little shovel carried in my pack hadn't been used. My waterproof wristwatch with battery-lit face, showed 6:00 am. Whether we climbed the glacier today or turned back, we needed to get up, eat breakfast, and pack. "Let's do it."

"Look at the waterfall." Matt's voice wafted up to us again. I stuck my head and shoulders out of our front flap to see the guys' tent tipped on its side. A puddle from their tent became a waterfall cascading to the meadow far below. Matt bragged: "We had two inches of water on the floor."

My son and grandson faced their dilemma with mixed temperaments, and 26 years difference in age. Nathan's well-known morning grouchiness, and Uncle Matt's longtime early-morning schedule qualified them as a mismatched couple. Except for their brown eyes, they didn't even look like relatives.

Brown-eyed tent mates, Nancy and I coalesced quite well, but certainly not much dryer. Inside tent-pockets held clean, but wet clothes for the day. My tiny notebook with first-day notes sagged from spongy ink blurs so I gave up on writing notes and poems. Rooting out dry clothes, deep down in my backpack, took all my energy. My limp sleeping bag slid into a big plastic bag. I hoped to dry it later in the sun.

What sun? Morosely, our crew put on ponchos, or garbage-bag substitutes, to begin morning motions in the drizzle. Lauren and Judy lowered their backpacks from a no-bear-climbing tree. Nancy hunted up our bear-proof food container from its pine-grove hiding place. We started breakfast in the same spot we had eaten our celebration dinner the night before, but had forgotten that joy of accomplishment. We were the only campers at Larch Knob.

Instead of a mountain lookout, our site resembled a steamy soup kitchen, wrapped in fog. As leader, I suggested, "Let's make a decision at ten."

No one else had much to say, besides grunts and nods. I wondered what we'd do for two hours in this spitting rain. Would we try to climb the glacier? If we back-tracked to cross that logjam bridge in the rain, we might make it to our starting-spot trailhead. Then we'd have to hitchhike to the B&B where Grandpa planned to spend his second night.

Who would pick up six hikers with soggy packs, muddy boots and grumpy dispositions? Suppose a motorist offered to take two or three of us? Would we split up? How would we find the B&B without an address? Would there be room for us, anyway? Wouldn't we feel cheated or wimpy about giving up? What kind of an anniversary gift was this trip anyway? Where was the holy hilarity? The spirited escape?

We couldn't climb the glacier in the rain with one ice ax, that no one knew how to use, and no crampons. At the outfitting store that sold me our freeze-dried food, I had looked at the grid of steel spikes called a crampon. The clerk showed me how to clamp the grid onto the sole of a boot. He admitted he had never used them and didn't know why they weren't called "clamp-ons."

The snow that glowed had promised favors, glory, love and care. Did we make that up? In this morning's mist we could see no mountains or meadows, and could barely focus on our breakfast. My compass skills might be called for, after all. What was that deviation from true North – seventeen degrees, east or west?

The three camp stoves sputtered to heat water for our metal cups of tea that would warm our hands. Judy offered me some cereal: "Hold this hot bowl."

That was as comforting as my stomach's acceptance of the warm oatmeal. An emergency Mealpak bar waited for me in the bear-proof container. Since we couldn't cook in a storm, I needed to move that meal to a convenient pocket for times of desperation. Its contents of milk, malt, corn, barley, and much more, had satisfied my hunger when I tested one at home. Unfortunately, I hadn't convinced any of my hikers to bring such emergency provisions.

Responsibility for five people–my nearest and dearest–stranded in snowy wilderness, I crumbled under the cloak of being leader. All of my muscles drooped. Nerves tightened like the wires in my newly-tuned spinet piano at home.

In John Mc Phee's book about this area, he describes an official sign, one mile out on the trail from Holden Village, that warns: "You are now entering Glacier Peak Wilderness Area." We were in that wilderness, and in a dilemma.

The Hardest Part

Blisters aren't the worst thing
about backpacking it's the manual
gas-stove directions translated from Swedish
about nipple cup cleaning needle
and regulating valve-key.

Just let me lace my boots
to stride onto that trail.
Don't warn me about a safety valve
in filler cap that *acts* if pressure
becomes too high acts up? acts stupid?

Ready I angle my rain proofed hat
but there are more stove instructions
keep it out of draughts (like in beer?)
warm stove with your hands to avoid
flaming yellow blazing flames.

I check topo map and compass
worry about our planned meals.
Must I sleep with the stove in my armpit
for a hot breakfast? At dinnertime should
I massage it with my frozen fingers? How
about mittens for the stove and for me?

I pick up heavy bottle of fuel
try to pour through one-inch funnel
manual says warmed gas trickles through nipple
into cup which ignites with waterproof match.

I grab my hiking stick
to leave such worries in camp
but directions insist *burner be kept free from*
soot deposit and the burner crown is well
screwed in. Ahhhh those Swedes...

Read between their lines: this
campstove doesn't want to rough it
take it to the ritz order up satin sheets.

barbara marysdaughter

Chapter Five
It's All Worthwhile

Day Two of Backpack

Climb Spider Glacier (a coulair,
or corridor of ice) to Spider Gap 7100'
(saddle between Chiwawa 8459'
and Dumbell mountains) 8407'

Snowfield descent to Lyman Valley 2000'
View Lyman's alpine-glacier toe at 6000'
Glacier type 3 – melts in 10-50 yrs.
Post Little Ice Age, (CE 1430-1866)

6 mi. to Lower Lyman campsite 5507'

The rain stopped about eight in the morning. Across the whiteness of Spider Glacier, Nathan's voice boomed like low trombone notes. "Let's go."

Blonde curls escaped from Lauren's bandana as she hoisted her pack. "Come on."

Sun shone on ice-carved peaks surrounding the snow-blanketed glacier. Rocky cliffs jutted out from snowdrifts tucked like comforters around these mountainous chins and sub-alpine trees. Bright glare devoured the tiny specks we had become. The sparkle shot through my squinty eyelids. This giant tongue of whitest-white beckoned us to poke around the corner up to the Gap.

Raingear came off; sunglasses went on. Divine consensus moved all our molecules upwards. The sun shone on our crew, held us in love like the glowing snow banks promised the night before.

"See those big dish-shapes?" Nathan called out. "The center might be thin. Stay away from them."

"OK."

Everyone had their "trail legs" after one day of hiking. Brother and sister skipped or flew up the steep slope to disappear around the corner. "Hey!" I yelled: "What about staying together?"

Two sisters and one brother (they called themselves "the original Johnsons"), and me, their mother/leader tackled the dazzling mile-long glacier. Filling its concave spillway, Spider Glacier pulled us up to see its wonders. That's when my memory kicked in: "What about Ranger Ken's alternate plan?"

"Where is his trail?" asked Nancy who had been persuaded to hike with us, only after Ranger Ken suggested a "safe way." His route took us away from the dangerous glacier. I looked above at sharp peaks piercing the snow. "Where could Ken's trail be?"

At home, that alternative route had sounded like the safe solution for us, and brought Nancy back on our hike. For weeks, I had studied Ranger Ken's topo map to learn the route.

At home in my loft-office, surrounded by peaks of the Santa Lucia Range, I had admired Cerro Alto at 2500 feet. But then I heard gunfire from the gnome, one-fourth mile away by winding road to shared easement, and yearned for this glacial wilderness. Now I couldn't translate those studies of Ken's route into reality.

Onward. Perfect weather prevailed, not too cold and full of promise. We followed our Hansel and Gretel contingent, knowing the mealpak bar should make fine "breadcrumbs." I tapped the bulge in my pocket where my emergency food awaited.

Like the claims of my grandchildren, and that happy camper in Spider Meadow, our glacier climb started easy. Matt used the ice ax as a walking stick. Nancy and I had old ski poles and Judy used a tree-branch. I worried about Judy's asthma.

Ten years previously she had given up flute playing when she ran out of air. She took up the viola instead, and took her medicine. Judy never looked back or complained. She biked and hiked. But what about climbing a glacier up to 7100 feet?

My three grown children and I proceeded like shorebirds at the beach. We skittered about, showed individuality with different paths. It was peaceful work. We were the only people in existence: no animal tracks, no neighbors.

Matt pulled ahead as we three women labored on this tangible masterpiece of glory and majesty and wonder. The enticing glacier beckoned us upward with a bigness that allowed each of us to have our own empire of whiteness.

Yet a dreaded task awaited us at the top. Descending that steep snowfield on the other side of the Gap scared me, more than climbing. Ranger Ken's alternate route had avoided that steep descent. In my pack a postcard, with the ranger's address on it, thanked him for our success with his alternate way. I never thought we would ignore his advice.

Judy, Nancy and I followed our glacial roadway around the corner. Blue sky backgrounded tiny silhouettes of Nathan and Lauren, already at the crest of Spider Gap. Matt climbed close behind them. Too easy, too quick, they had already conquered the glacier. The next time I looked, Nathan galloped down without his backpack, to this steep part where we three women traversed, all in a line. We fired questions at him.

"Any dangers?"

" How's the view at the top?"

"What about the descent?"

"It's all worthwhile." Nathan sounded like a hiking convert. "Wait till you see the view, Grandma. I'll carry your pack to the top."

"I'll let you do that."

Nathan whisked my pack up and onward. He was gone before I could thank him. He'd fit into the intentional community, I believed, that we headed for. My hate-to-be-a-wimp impulses had disengaged because of his offer. With a new lightness in my step, I could fly to the Gap, maybe the moon. Without the pack, my confidence multiplied and ordered my boots to march forcefully without fear. I could show those doubters who argued I looked too little to climb mountains, too fragile with my small bones. But I have strong legs, and a belief that determined old ladies are unstoppable.

Nancy moved along before me on the steep incline through meringue-consistency snow that allowed good toeholds. Judy was in front. Each footstep held securely. We ignored the temptation to look down.

My feet rejoiced in double, wool socks. Seattle Tom, the Spider Gap hiker from REI, had recommended these $15 liners and outer socks when I visited him at the headquarter store. Tom also suggested sliding down the snowfield as the best way to handle the Lyman side. "Send your pack down, and follow it. It will be fun."

"I'll never do that," I had told him. "Too dangerous."

"If the snowfield isn't too big, you can skirt it by rock hopping," Tom had said. "Of course, it is really steep."

"How steep?"

"Steep," he had answered with a shrug.

Our gang of three crested the Gap. Judy threw down her pack, opened her arms in triumph, with no apparent breathing problems. All six of us climbers celebrated, embraced the moment, each other, and the glacier we had climbed. We stared at the other-worldly scenery of Lyman Glacier, an older, bigger glacier in the next valley, not on our schedule to climb. In fact, with global warming, the glacier could be melted in ten years.

Holden's Operations Department watches such things. Melted-glacier water feeds the village hydro-power plant, as the least intrusive of electric systems. But to come back in a decade to find this gorgeous piece of ice gone, melted; that seems too fast. And what about flooding, bridges washed out?

But the steep snowfield captured my rapt attention. This snow-slide dropped off, almost straight down. Boulders, the size of freight cars, peeked out of the snow. How would I slide down without hitting them? My pack might bound over the edge. So could I.

Until then, atop Spider Glacier, our group balanced on the cusp of the slippery slope. Happy to be there, we rested, snacked, and bragged about climbing this challenge that seemed impossible three hours earlier. If only Grandpa could be smoke-signaled or cell-phoned or satellite-alerted to our triumph. I hoped he enjoyed his freedom from daily harassment, like I did.

"And Tyler might want to know," said Judy whose 14-year-old was home with his father.

"Can't you see Tyler," I suggested, "biking the loops and curves on Lyman Glacier?"

Our crew lounged on the Gap, gaped at a panorama that taught us the history of Lyman Lakes Valley from rounded basin to mountain slopes chewed by the retreating glacier. With stark contrasts of snow and peaks, subtle shifting planes carved by ice, the glacier became an Ansel Adams photograph. We looked and looked and looked at the glacier, and glanced at our steep 1000-foot down slope. We needed to slide down into that black-and-white picture.

Nathan and Lauren pushed their packs and followed on imaginary sleds. Their speed did not seem too fast or out of control. Every fifty feet or so they repeated the process. It looked easy. Matt and Nancy tried it. So did Judy. What was this old lady waiting for?

A shove, and my backpack started. It slowly bumped its way down and stopped. I sat down on the snow, pushed myself with heels and ski pole, and took off. Not too fast. No longer scared, I easily stopped at my pack. Our family excursion had become a Grandma Moses sledding party. Like Seattle Tom had said, it was fun.

Nancy tied our two packs together for a heavier, quicker descent. She held its strap like a dog's leash and bounced along behind it. Amazed and confident, I became sloppy in selecting my next sit-down runway. I slipped. Bang. "Ouch!"

How can snow be so hard? Tailbone tweaked and body took off on a fast track. Ski pole waved in the air and refused to dig into the snow to slow me down. My boot heels couldn't grab anything. The slope steepened. My course aimed at Matt who stood in the last stretch before the rocky cliff. The drop-off.

"I'm out of control. Out of control. Can't stop."

Was my speed 100 miles an hour? I couldn't focus on anyone but Matt who watched me getting closer and closer. "Don't stab me with that pole."

My downfall felt like an ill-fated luge run. This wasn't the kind of unstoppable old lady I carried in my mind. Clawing the snow with my bare left hand, my body burned with fear. That hand, like reins on a horse, steered me to a halt at Matt's feet. I didn't puncture my son after all.

"Oh my God." I looked at the drop to the valley floor, my destination if I hadn't stopped. "Holy Moses."

"You OK?" Matt asked.

"Yes." I spoke in a small, little-girl's voice.

Our family, saved from disasters, real and imagined, walked together to the edge of the snowfield. We were finished with that, heading for the safety of dirt, earth, holy ground.

I was surprised that no one else heard the melted snow gurgling beneath us, and asked, "Don't you hear that water?"

"Hear what?" Matt and Nathan were already on dry land.

Lauren and I broke through the crust at the same time. Our legs dropped into piercing-cold melted snow, flowing fast, up to mid-calf. I gasped. "Woooooo."

Nancy and Judy, about a yard away from us, looked surprised. "What's going on?"

"Yeeeeeeeeeee," was my granddaughter's response.

We both stepped out without missing a beat, like experienced mountaineers. "Just some ancient glacial water," I said.

Lunching in the sun, drying camping gear and relaxing on a gravely hill, Lauren and I took off our cold, wet boots and socks. As we wrung out clothes and sleeping bags to spread on the warm rock, I told her about hikers who get soaked at the beginning of a glacier climb: "At the end of the day, I've read, they have to chop their frozen boots off, to save their feet."

"No way." Lauren wiggled her toes and leaned back on the warm boulder we had chosen for our victory lunch and rest. We snacked on dried apricots, stale bagels, bits of cheese and nearly emptied our water bottles. The air had a chill in it. Lauren and I searched for dry socks in our packs.

As a group, we contemplated the scenery, dominated by a turquoise-colored upper lake with floating icebergs, framed by layers of Lyman Glacier, almost identical with the Hollywood Bowl. I wondered how the glacier looked in 1900 when, according to geological studies, the glacier was 70 percent bigger.

Lyman's icy majesty invited fantasies of an incredible glacial cirque, an amphitheatre with an audience sitting in box seats on delineated tiers of ice. We could almost hear an orchestra tuning up. While an opera production practiced on the apron of the stage, ice-skaters whirled on the mirrored lake. All in our sleepy daydream.

In groggy sequences, we composed music, costumed dancers, built scenes and cast formal-dressed, bejeweled audiences for a theatre of the absurd. Our collective minds invented, while gastric juices digested our food.

With my scraped tailbone, I chose my sitting rock carefully. We all rested and communed with this relic glacier from the Last Ice age, surrounded by barren desolation. And we talked to each other. Nancy relived that last steep incline going up Spider Glacier: "I looked down and became terrified, figuring that if we slipped, we would end up in one of those dishes with the thin crust in the middle, slip through the glacier to the rushing water below, like the disasters at Mt. Hood. Our bodies wouldn't be dug up for 5000 years."

"But you kept going," I said.

Nancy smiled. She had fallen in the creek, and continued on. With her horses at home, she has had scary moments, particularly in jumping class. On that Whitney climb when she was 11, she turned green from altitude sickness but reached the top.

"Our family must have an adventure gene," I said, "and nerves of steel."

Matt told us he delivered some Dutch uncle advice to his nephew at the top of the Gap. "I said, 'Nathan, you should quit being so grouchy and be a little more helpful.'"

That's when Nathan came down and relieved me of my pack. That's when he proclaimed: "It's all worthwhile."

Over the years we have stretched our capabilities to weave these memories of adventures that tested our abilities. This trip was part of a long line of coping, going back to Ted's Boundary Waters canoe trip with high school buddies. He told me about it on our first date. He said he nearly froze every night because his sleeping bag was just a liner, with no warmth. Yet I was attracted to the whole idea and wanted to go on trips like that with him.

Did books influence me or is it something I ate? Are Ted and I genetically adventuresome?

Did we pass that trait on to the next generation?

Our experienced crew found a tramped-down hiking trail, ready to send us on our six-mile hike to Lower Lyman campsite. It showed us snow patches shaped like golf-course greens. Huge, rectangular granite slabs had been forced off the mountains by the glacier and appeared like architectural accents in a Japanese garden. Or enormous gravestones. Were they tangible evidence of 600 years of combat with gravity, destroying 70 percent of the glacier? What would Ted say, with his interest in geology?

Then I thought about bears again.. One of the tour books claimed "Around Holden Village, there may be more bears running around than Lutherans."

At our pine-scented campsite near Lower Lyman Lake, we set up quickly like the seasoned packers we had become. Lauren brought in kindling and middling firewood on a sledge she made from a fallen log. "Look! Campfire tonight."

We gathered around Lauren's fire, sitting on logs, a painful seat for my sore tailbone. Nathan wanted to get to Holden's pool hall. "Why can't I hike all the way to Holden tonight, and not have to camp?"

"You're not going to do that," Judy said. "There are bears out there."

Examples of bear attacks invaded my mind: "One tooth-mark, an inch from a child's eye was deep enough to reach his brain. Black bears can kill a cow with one bite to the neck."

Nancy brought out her book, *God of Small Things*. We took turns reading about the night when the children drowned. Feeling reasonably safe from such disasters, if Nathan didn't bolt away into the woods, we stayed late at the fire that Lauren tended. It was a civilized thing to do, almost hypnotic, to be read to. The next day we would walk out of the wilderness together into a little pocket of civilization.

Around midnight something galumphed through the campsite. All family members except me got up, took out their flashlights to scan tents and woods with bright beams. I stayed in the tent and listened to nervous talking and giggling. How could they laugh? They hadn't read the bear book. I should have sent them the gruesome stories along with those glorious write-ups, and guidebook photos.

They went back to bed convinced it had been a bear in camp. An hour later, thrash, clump, galumph. The same crew turned out, same flashlights, but groggier chatter with less hilarity.

Cold, old, tired and worried, I sat up in my sleeping bag and pulled it tightly around my neck. What would my brave family do if they saw a bear biting my neck? Wasn't banging pots and pans, the thing to do? But our cooking utensils were stored far from the tents, as suggested in the bear book. So was all our food.

But sometimes bears sniff out a flavorful toothpaste. My hand reached out to the tent pocket that held my toiletry kit. There sat the little tube of toothpaste, perfuming the tent.

Moods Of Snow On Spider Glacier

Midsummer midnight snow patches on
slopes surrounding eagle-nest campsite
glow in bio-luminescence.
How well do we know snow?

Powder icy mushy strong enough
for footholds in snowfield fantasy of
frozen yogurt soft and hard-packed
ice cream-cover with reflective sky
colors on slow-paced Spider Glacier.

How slow is a well-paced glacier that
covers rushing scouring glacial-milk
below crusty capped crevasses?

At dawn six of us confront top layer
of snow bowls with centers weak
enough to plunge climbers into secret
water beneath whipped creamy surface.

No one speaks the unspeakable.
No step misses a toehold we dig
boot heels into steep slopes
climb single file in glacial-time
to gape at gap in triumph.

Our knowledge of luminescence and
glacial secrets remains a glimmer
we don't know snow at all.

barbara marysdaughter

Chapter Six
Angels Of the Ball Field

Day Three of Backpack

Lower Lyman campsite 5507'
follow Railroad Creek
8 miles to Holden Village 3307'

Morning brought us evidence about our midnight visitor. Fresh deer-tracks crossed the tent area. So it wasn't a predacious bear. Still, a huge rutting buck crashing into one's tent is not a pretty thing.

Our trip began to have a guardian-angel glow to it. The glacier climb had worked for us. My slide down the snowfield stopped before I reached the edge, or stabbed my son with the ski pole. The weather fixed itself and we hiked our grand finale in good spirits.

Angels hang out in the mountains, I like to believe, to work with people who need them. Instead of astral creatures in billowing sheets, angels might look like the jolly glacier-climber in Spider Meadow who warned us about the dangerous creek-crossing. Angels are good friends who support our efforts and are always ready to listen to us.

Judy set up our bagels, jam, coffee, tea, and oatmeal on a fallen trunk at the lake's edge. We basked in the sun and celebrated the sweetness of jam and seriousness of oatmeal. Matt took out his fishing pole to give Lyman Lake a try. Somebody had told him the fish up here were naive.

Maybe we were, too, in many ways.

The only other lake-site camper, a 30-ish man in shorts, passed by our breakfast log on his way to Cloudy Pass.

"Hear that buck last night?"

"Sure did."

Instead of chatting about intruders, trails, maps and adventures, all of us had to swat black flies who had arrived for breakfast. The hiker picked up his walking stick. "Have to get moving. Don't let the flies get a hold on you."

Dreaded black flies silently drilled into our necks, arms, and legs, for the initial sting. Long-lasting red spots informed us to jump, dance around and get ready in a hurry.

The trail to Holden led us through musty jungle-growth shades of green to dry cottonwood and willows to gray conifers. Serious, but not hairy creek-crossings slowed down our rush to the finish line. Glacial-green Hart Lake, a mountain tarn fed by Lyman Glacier, provided a lovely shore for lunch. We ran its half-century-old water through our camping filter for a pure, but flat taste.

The sun bore down. I unzipped lower sections of my hiking pants. To slip the pantlets over my feet, I had to remove my boots. Such a liberating moment insisted I put on sandals for the end of our hike. "And more skin for the flies," I moaned. "It should make them smile."

The rest of our group became skittish horses swishing flies away. I still needed to tie my boots onto my pack frame, so I said, "Go ahead. I'll be along soon."

"Mom, you can't finish this hike alone." Matt winced as he stood up again in his steel-toed boots. "Won't be breaking any speed records in these. I'll wait for you."

To mosey along with Matt was comforting. Glowing with the idea that we were in no hurry, but still wanting to end the misery soon, we quizzed the first hikers we saw. "How much further?"

A family with two children stopped and the mother said, "Two and a half miles."

Two young men came along next. They said, "Fifteen minutes."

After a half-hour of hiking, we took another opinion: "One mile to the sign."

"We're going to make it, Matt."

My son grunted. Not much for chit-chat, especially when he was hurting, he didn't want to talk about anything. Matt, the motorcycle racer, the cross-country dirt bike trophy winner dragged along.

Footgear and socks either propel, or torture us hikers. I knew this, but had changed into blister-producing strap-sandals, without socks. My naive, devil-may-care self did that. Matt and I approached the *Leaving Wilderness/Entering Civilization* sign, next to a wooden bench that tempted me.

"Can't sit," Matt said.

We kept going. I said, "Nathan's probably played a couple games of pool already."

Certain trees and curves in the trail looked familiar to me, from fifteen years previously when running these paths each morning. Pine needles still perfumed the air. Matt and I approached the old ball field where forty years ago, miners had games and picnics with their families. People gathered around an old bulletin board by the side of the trail, and turned to face us.

"Matt, there's our welcoming committee."

"Yeh, right."

It wasn't Ted, nor any members of our family, but a group of men and women we didn't know, and a couple of children. They looked like people at a church picnic, or miner's ballgame, just hanging out, watching us stumble in at last. Two of them waved.

I turned around to see who they were greeting. No one hiked behind us. I kept going, looking for my husband. If it's only one mile, wouldn't Ted walk out to greet us? The people at the sign applauded.

"Matt, they're clapping for us."

"Right. I just want to throw away these boots."

The people at the ballpark called out, "One mile to the village."

"Hey, this is Holden's ticker-tape welcome," I whispered to my son. "They are angels." I tried to carry my pack with ease, ignored aching heels, stood taller and walked with faked assurance. Matt and I never slowed down or asked how the angels knew about us. We approached the finish line with two questions:

"Where's Ted?"

"When can I take a shower?"

I should have asked the ball field angels what was for dinner. To the right of our trail appeared another seductive bench, carved out of a huge tree trunk, facing the curve of Railroad Creek. Environmentalist Dave Brower had looked at this same waterway decades ago. He described it as "one God-awful mess, with piles of rusted cars, ore carts, and flakes of corrugated iron." Holden had cleaned up the creek since those mining days.

We could have floated down in the mist of the churning water like two Cleopatras. Hiking five miles in sandals forced my heels to complain louder. Changing to shorts attracted more flies. Bad decisions. To float in that sparkling creek, in spite of its boulders and whirl pools, appealed to me.

Matt and I trudged past the creek and its tempting bench. The trail widened and dipped like a roller-coaster. On the up slope stood a man in a white straw hat. I had given Ted a hat like that for his birthday. It seemed years since I had seen him instead of three days. He looked civilized and clean. I whispered to Matt, "I think that's Dad."

"Yep."

"Ted." He ran down the slope. Matt and I collided with him. "We made it," I said. "We all did it. Everything worked out."

In the crush of father, mother, son, packs, hiking sticks, and words and hugs, one thing piled on top of another. Laughing interrupted kissing. I needed to sit down and cry. Matt said he wanted to shed his boots.

I asked Ted, "Where's the rest of our family?"

"Everybody's unpacking," Ted reported, "taking showers, starting laundry–except Nathan"

"Did you see him come in?".

"I never saw him. Judy says he's playing pool."

"How long have they been here?"

"Ten minutes."

"Not too shabby." I gave Matt a playful jab on his shoulder, and another one for Ted. We started walking again. I ignored my feet and my delirium that I was a war hero coming home in one piece. "What are we having for dinner?"

"An outdoor picnic with Sloppy Joes, made from lentils."

I muttered the old quote: "Came here as a Lutheran and left as a lentil," and laughed like a drunk, stumbling down the road. I asked Ted if he knew about the greeting committee at the ball field.

"No, I haven't talked to anyone."

I sighed; how typical of Ted.

"I don't know who your greeters were," he added.

"Angels," I whispered. "Angels."

What did I know about angels? And how did we make their A-list? Could they deal with sociopath neighbors? Were they guardians who could see through them? Did they have names like Raphael, Michael, Gabriel? Angela?

In a haze of glory, mother and son came out of the wilds with civilized Ted, past the ore-crushing factory with rusted beams twisted toward the sky. Then came mining barracks converted into lodges. We stopped at Lodge One.

Ted put my pack on the porch. "This is where we will stay, but we can't move in yet."

"Why not?"

"The woman who is moving out thought we weren't due till six." Ted checked his watch. "It's three-thirty. Wait here while I take Matt to his room in Lodge Three."

I slumped on the front steps, unbuckled my sandals. "OK."

They followed the brick sidewalk up the hill while Ted explained, "You and Nancy are sharing a room."

I perked up and called out to Matt. "That will take you back forty years."

A glow of togetherness swept over me. In our individual ways, our family loved each other. I breathed in the moist, moldy-leaf good-earth smell of the flower beds near the porch and smiled inwardly, satisfied, anticipating a great two-day visit.

Other Lodge One residents on the porch with me, sat in the swing and various chairs. I imagined they were impressed by this old lady who had hiked in, but not enough to offer her a chair. Bent over, examining my sore heels, I felt something jump on my back, bigger than a black fly but smaller than a bear. I tried to swat it with my hand. As the brown and black fur ball ran off, I leaped up. The chipmunk turned to stare at me with fearless eyes.

The young people on the porch, soon to be my neighbors, paid no attention. A man on a ladder, painting overhang trim, didn't notice either. I sat down on the steps and watched the chippie circle to stage another attack. My tired body slid back to the wall where Ted had placed our luggage and my pack. I leaned against this impressive pile of stuff and yearned to take a shower. I felt sticky, sweaty, dirty, harassed by a chipmunk and barred from everyone else, in my imaginary holding tank.

A husky young woman in bib overalls arrived at the steps, now free of chipmunks. She pushed a dolly loaded with boxes. She didn't see me but greeted a young woman in a bright-print long skirt, carrying a bedroll and coming down the stairway from the second floor.

"Is that all?" asked the woman with the dolly, probably a volunteer Maverick. They do a variety of jobs required by Holden's 300 guests and 100 staff members.

"Just a few more things," said the slim woman with long red hair.

Could that be the woman moving out of our room? Surely she would recognize me as part of the Johnson twosome waiting to move in. Wouldn't she welcome me to the civilized community of these porch people, dressed in clean clothes, gazing at Alp-like scenery surrounding us?

She walked away with the other woman who pushed the loaded dolly. The chipmunk watched me slumping next to the wall. I considered putting on my boots to squash him. Ted returned to report Judy and Nancy taking turns battling others for use of laundry equipment.

I told him, "The woman has probably moved out of our room. Do you have the key?"

"No one has a key – Holden policy for forty years," he answered. "No keys. I'll go up and knock on room 19 and see if anyone's there." He stopped on the second step. "We have to go to a staff meeting right after dinner."

I groaned, and marveled how clean he looked. Ted quickly bounded back down the steps: "The door's wide open. Everything seems to be gone. Let's move in."

We did. Immediately, I sniffed out the huge pine tree trunk that grew close to our one window. Ted opened the medicine cabinet over our tiny wash basin. We saw things she had left behind. Like magic, the red-haired lady appeared in the doorway. "I haven't moved out yet, and I still need to vacuum and clean everything."

"Do you want us to take our things out into the hallway?" I tried not to sound sarcastic while picking up the hateful pack. "All I really want is to take a shower."

She studied me. "Yes, why don't you take a shower? They are at the end of the hallway. I just need about 20 minutes."

Grabbing a towel, soap and clean clothes, I limped down the hall, anticipating warm water pouring over my body to cleanse and soothe. Ted left to see how our daughters survived their laundry battle.

What about those angels waving and greeting us at the ball field? Maybe this was the real world where angels are invisible, I thought, and walked into the men's shower room.

A large woman raced down the hall, calling to me, "Oh, the women's showers are on the left side."

I came out of the men's room and stood in the hallway.

"And be sure you turn on the exhaust fan, or the steam will trigger the fire alarm," she added and went back to her room. Civilization seemed complicated, or was she another angel?

All the chipmunks in Glacier Peak Wilderness attended Holden's sloppy-Joe-lentils picnic-supper. Our family group, showered and calmed down from the laundry wars, sat on a low retaining wall and in big wooden chairs on the lawn. We enjoyed the grassy village green under a big pine that held the official bell. The Holden bell signified "healing of the earth," according to a nearby plaque. It called us to meals, classes and activities. This metallic bell became a strong center, or open door, ringing every evening for vespers.

That's the gathering that all villagers are asked to attend every night. None of our family were church goers at this time, in spite of years of confirmation, participation in youth groups, choir, council and social activities. I didn't know who in our family would attend vespers.

Nathan left the pool hall to join us for supper. Hundreds of picnickers on this Village Green protected their savory sloppy-joes from the chipmunk contingent. Lauren swatted a chippie coming over her shoulder and arm, heading for her plate. She connected. The animal soared through the air.

"Wow."

"A flying chipmunk."

No one else seemed to notice. Learning to live with chipmunks may be part of the Holden intentionality. We, the weary, griping hikers had hoped to sit down at a table inside after three days of sitting on logs and rocks. My hiking team treated the oniony, garlicy, vegetarian sloppy-joes with contempt. However, the meal brought me ecstasy and I particularly appreciated the fresh green salad.

Nathan hurried back to the pool hall. Lauren returned to reading *Les Miserables*. Judy called the village a "cult we don't belong to." But she went down to the pottery studio anyway to talk to the artist in charge.

Ted and I wanted them to like Holden during their two-day stay. My worn-out glacier-climbers pointed out how long they had had to wait in the ice cream line, the struggle to wedge laundry into the rush-hour traffic for equipment, and that they certainly weren't going to vespers tonight. None were interested in the sauna or hot tub either.

Would they have felt differently if they had been cheered by the angels of the ball field? Matt said he didn't think so. He wanted to go to bed early, too. Ted and I trundled off to our first staff meeting.

In the huge Fireside Room, with overhanging balcony for additional attendees who looked down over the edge, we found two empty seats. Without a cushion, my chair proved painful for my dinged tailbone. In front, were two women running the meeting. One of them was the beautifully-dressed red-haired former-inhabitant of our room.

On the board behind them were questions that newcomers should answer when introducing themselves: name, home state, volunteer job, and favorite movie. Movie? None came to mind, good or bad. I felt like the rest of my family: just let me sleep.

One hundred volunteers gathered in the room, plus some full-time year-round employees. The din of voices crushed me after the silence of the wilds. When called upon, I stood up in our back corner of the packed meeting room, surprised that I could raise my body to a vertical position, and speak. "May I say something different, than answers to those questions?"

The room became quiet. The dark-haired woman, Rose Ann, hesitated only a second before she said, "Of course."

Loving her for that, I claimed her as another angel and began, "I'm not myself tonight. Just came off of a 20-mile three-day hike to get here this afternoon, and can't think of a single movie I like or dislike. I'll be OK by tomorrow.

"But I'm still named Barbara Johnson, still married to fellow volunteer Ted Johnson, still live in California, and am still going to work as a gardener."

I sat down to a quietness, and seriously asked myself who I really was.

The next new staffer answered the required questions. So did Ted when it was his turn.

During announcements, Holden's co-director Dianne said money had been stolen from one of the rooms. "In our forty-year tradition of open doors, nothing has ever been stolen before. This is troubling to the whole community. We offer secrecy to the person who brings the money back. And no punishment."

The audience became silent like at a funeral. Dianne continued. "If no one comes forward, staff members have offered to donate enough money to reimburse the victim of this theft. We all believe it is important to live here as trusting and trusted people."

Yes, I liked what she said. She spoke like an angel created from light, like those at the ballpark. I expected to meet more angels in the rhythms of the next day.

Enchilada Casserole

Recipes are from *Cook Boldly*, 5th edition; Editors: Ginger Flynn, Chantal Hulet, Clover Thurk; Chelan Printing Co., Chelan, WA

(AUTOGRAPHED by kitchen crew, Aug. 2002: *Especially yummy with extra cheese!* Adriann)

1 2/3 C pinto beans, uncooked
1 C white rice, uncooked
2/3 C onions, diced
1 tsp garlic, minced
1 tsp cumin
½ tsp ground coriander
1/4 tsp chili powder
2 10-ounce cans tomato sauce
12 corn tortillas
1 ½ C corn
4 C Monterey-jack cheese, grated

Soak beans overnight. Cook beans until tender, about 1 hour.
Cook rice. To make sauce, sauté onions until soft, add spices and tomato sauce. Simmer until hot. Combine rice, beans and sauce. In a greased 9 X 13" pan, layer ingredients in the following order: tortillas, rice and bean mixture, corn and cheese. Repeat. Cover with foil and bake at 350 degrees for 45 minutes. Serve with chips and salsa.

Part Three: The Escape

Chapter Seven
Where Doors Are Never Locked

Vesper from Olympus now at last is raising his long-looked-for light....The evening has come; rise up. Catullus, 54 BCE

Lunch had to be explained to our "non-members-of-this-cult" family. The meal consisted of one dish, incredible as that seems: plain rice. To understand such Holden-place-apart programs may be difficult with only 40 hours' exposure. Our children and grandchildren had slept nearly half of that limited time.

Recovering from the aches and pains of our hike, we each had to prepare for the next saga of our stories. Ted and I were grateful for our longer stay. The rest of our family were leaving the next morning. We sat down at the table for eight, taking up seven of the seats. Thick air, with its moistness of cooked rice, settled upon us.

"Sorry this has to be your only lunch here." Ted included each of our hiking team in his comment.

The nearly bare table settings offered a steaming bowl of white rice, that wafted the starchy aroma throughout the dining hall among the 200 people at the first setting. Another dish on each table held a stick of bright yellow butter. Proud of it, I held up the dish. "To put on your rice!"

Skeptical looks greeted my enthusiasm. Our family surveyed the usual set-up of plates and utensils. A little rack in the center held paper napkins. Glasses awaited ice water from the pitcher. I agreed with Holden's Wednesday lunch idea and longed to share that mission with my family. This identical meal came around every week to embrace issues of the world, including the fact that some people starve. Money saved on this lunch, thousands each year, buys food for the hungry in areas near the village.

Ted pointed to the buffet. "There's bread and peanut butter over there, if you need it."

"No salad?"

"Where's that famous Holden bread?"

"No cookies?"

"No pie?"

This paltry meal spoke to the weariness and soreness of us hikers who had been on a self-inflicted diet ruled by what we could carry. Perhaps with this limited meal – although we could have all the rice we wanted

– we gained a glimmer of what starvation is. Our family ate the offering, admitting that it was pretty good rice. Lauren took out her book and began reading. Nathan disappeared to play pool. Matt said he might go fishing. And we all planned to line up at three for ice cream.

Some villagers say you have to live here awhile to "get it," to understand what Holden is really about. To see this kind of a meal as a challenge to society's conscience, we can examine our overwhelming selfishness and materialism. An article in a Japanese news magazine emphasized egalitarianism and voluntary simplicity, as important Holden creeds.

Co-director Diane, wearing a casual pantsuit, finished lunch announcements with a happy message: "The money stolen last week from a villager's purse, something that has never happened during the 40 years of our no-locks policy..." She paused. "Has been returned!"

Applause, cheering, whistling, stomping on the floor, and hands slapping the tables erupted all over the room. I joined the hilarity. My family watched, listened and looked out of it.

Dianne's gentle plea the day before had literally paid off. The angels in the ballfield must have moved into the village to look right through us all. The guilty had owned up. Pounding the table in celebration along with the rest till my hands ached, this new-kid-in-the-village moved into the heart of our trusted, and trusting community. Wouldn't Holden villagers cheer Ted, too, if they understood his innocence, and wrongful arrest?

Here, we didn't lock our doors, and to feed the hungry we ate rice, and then ice cream.

First in line was a roundy little boy, and second was tall, skinny Ted, on his afternoon break from the carpentry shop. He said he had his first assignment measured and planned. "I'm making storage boxes for CDs in the library."

"Great," I said. "I haven't found my gardening boss yet."

The rest of our family came next in line, followed shortly by 20 or more rice-eaters behind us. Volunteer workers inside the parlor, amid a sweetness in the air, wrote current flavors on the board: Maple Nut, Death by Chocolate, Black Cherry and Raspberry Sorbet. Boxes of cones filled the back counters. A young woman at the cash register counted her money. Jerry, the czar of ice cream and a retired high school principal, directed the ice cream operation like a general on the battlefield. He wore an African free-flowing robe and rang a hand-bell before opening the door. The first-in-line boy's mother wedged in before Ted, saying, "How nice that we're first."

Nancy and Judy whispered to their father. "That's the cheeky lady from the laundry."

"She claimed all the machines for herself."

Our line brought us to volunteer scoopers who piled copious amounts onto our cones, all for seventy-five cents. "That's a single dip?"

"It's a Holden single," the smiling young man explained.

Sitting on the deck with other ice-cream eaters, including the calmed-down laundry queen, I asked our family, "How would you like working here as volunteers for a couple of weeks?"

"No way...Not for me..."

Our teenaged grandchildren and forty-ish children rejected the idea, but Ted, licking a Maple-nut cone, tried to convince them, "You'd get the free ice cream!"

Not interested. Our glacier-climbing party was over, balloons deflated, musicians packed up. They weren't buying Holden. Reared in a San Fernando Valley Lutheran church, they now have individual choice, the same freedom I sought.

I broke into another deck conversation: "Did I hear that you guys just did Spider Gap?"

One young men turned to look at me. I added, "We did it last week. How was it today?"

"No problem. We climbed part of Lyman Glacier, too."

"Great," I said and they turned away. The party really was over.

For the family farewell, Ted and I spruced up our cell-like room which would be our home base for the next four weeks. We threw stuff into the closet, camping gear in a corner, swept beds clear of clothing. Ted placed the one chair at our tiny built-in table. Paper napkins, Chardonnay Ted had brought in, plus left-over fruit juice and bagel-bits awaited our guests.

"Twin beds!" Judy said when she walked in.

"Yeah," I answered. "Is that anyway to celebrate an anniversary?"

Ted frowned. "We couldn't figure out how to shove them together. There isn't room."

"Sit down on the beds." I moved my pillow for a backrest and leaned gratefully against the wall. My tailbone was healing. We clinked glasses and toasted the wilderness, our successful encounter with it, and God-speed for the five leaving the next morning. We didn't talk about the rice-lunch or Holden creeds.

Judy, relaxing like around a campfire, told us, "When you guys had parties, Nancy and I used to angle the bathroom mirror, so we could watch you."

"You did?" I tried to remember what they might have seen.

Nancy jumped in. "Guests like the Meyers, told lots of good jokes. We spied on you having a good time, laughing, drinking wine, and slathering butter on sourdough bread."

Ted answered, "And we never noticed."

"Where was I?" asked Matt.

"In your beddy-bye," announced Nancy, his big sister by four years.

Lauren and Nathan laughed at their elders and moved on to what they had seen in the village:

"A T-shirt: Let it mellow if yellow; flush it down if brown."

"Bathroom signs: Condoms go in the bio-waste buckets."

"Did you see the condoms on the table, just down the hall?"

"The sign said: Wear them."

"The Sexual Etiquette list: No means NO, Be discreet, and so on."

What would have inspired them most if they had stayed for four weeks? The conversation flowed on:

"No alcohol or tobacco is sold here, is it?"

"No," Ted answered, "but they can order it whenever the boat goes out."

"So is this party legal?"

"As long as we're discreet," Ted answered. "But if you're caught using illegal drugs, you're asked to leave."

"And they don't sell pop or candy bars," Matt noted.

"The handbook says this place isn't perfect," I reminded them. Like all of us, I thought, and tried to talk them into hot tub or sauna before bedtime. But everyone wanted to go to bed early again.

"That's OK." I said. "My work as a gardener begins tomorrow at six."

"Your boss found you?" asked Nancy.

"Yes, and she said workers can take time off to be with family, or for any class, or to send off departing guests."

"That's us," Judy said. "Tomorrow at ten."

After a redeeming, regular full dinner of enchiladas with all the trimmings, Ted and I bid good night to our kids and grandkids who wanted a long-night's sleep. We caught vespers, the informal, nightly worship session with good music and short message. The program pulled about 400 people every night into the Village Center.

At the lectern in front, a young woman called our names along with 20 or more new villagers. Ted and I stood up with the other newcomers to be welcomed. When the woman named each of our absent children and grandchildren, it was a bit of an ache that they weren't there. Yet they had come to the village to be with us – first traveling up the coast together, hiking over the glacier, and spending two days schmoozing in the village. We were satisfied

In Andrew Newberg's book, *Why God Won't Go Away*, he claims "God is hardwired into the human brain." He says that there is a natural yearning for a higher power, a comforter, an explanation. If so, our family would find their own creeds and answers. Some folks satisfy that yen with vespers, or Holden's unlocked-door policy, or one-dish meals on Wednesdays, and gatherings described as extravagant, absurd celebrations.

Wasn't it strange that our family's names were called out while they were up the hill, a block away, totally unaware? Could vespers be absurd to make a memorable point? And another thing, always on my mind, isn't the biblical teaching to love one's neighbors unreasonable, when neighbors vow destruction? Yet even Freud has cited love-thy-neighbor advice as "one of the ideal demands of civilized society."

The next day began at dawn for me, with tea and toast at the gardening meeting with gardeners John, Sadie and our boss, Jennifer, blonde and tall, looking like a model. She gave me sprinkling directions and a watering can for the 24 hanging flower-baskets in the village.

First thing, I mismanaged a flower box that overflowed onto porch furniture. My next struggle whipped kinked hoses around, to spray a surprised guest. Breakfast time-out gave me a chance to relax, with a rested family getting ready to re-enter their real lives. Time raced by like a speeded-up movie.

"Well, has it been a good anniversary so far?" asked Judy as we walked up the hill to get her luggage.

Stopping to look at her, I decided to tell her this: "Your father and I came together last night..."

"No, no," she said, throwing up her hands. "I don't want to hear that about my parents..." We both laughed so hard we staggered off the path.

At ten, Ted and I met the deportees at the bus-loading dock, on the main-street (the only *real* street). Nathan had to be yanked out of the pool hall. Lauren discovered a library next to the bus stop, dashed in and complained: "Two rooms full of books I haven't read yet."

Nancy had us line-up for a final group photo, but the delayed flash didn't work. Another departing guest offered to take the picture. The camera flashed and we thanked her. She told us she hated to leave because her daughter's birthday was Sunday.

"What's her name?" I asked.

"Sara. She works with the kitchen crew."

"I'll sing Happy Birthday to Sara," I promised.

A recycled yellow school bus pulled up to take passengers on the switch-backed trip to the boat landing. Fifty villagers gathered for this typical send-off. Four drummers beat out the rhythm that revved up our motors and emotions. Travelers lined up for the bus. Lauren and Nathan leaned out of the bus window. "We're saving seats for you guys," Lauren called to Matt, Nancy and Judy: "Come on."

Judy had one step on the bus when a woman directed a question, in a loud voice, to Ted and me. "Who is going to pay for these people?"

"You mean our children and grandchildren?" I asked.

"The ones with that woman with the pigtail."

"Oh, Judy paid long ago, with her credit card."

"We don't take credit cards."

"Then she wrote a check." We shouted this conversation over the heads of fellow villagers. "She made reservations last May, and paid then."

The drums stepped up the insistent rhythm. The woman must have been the village accountant, or truant officer. Had she noticed our family didn't attend vespers?

Ted caught Judy's attention before she disappeared into the bus and she came over. Judy explained to the woman how and when she paid. The bus driver tooted the horn. Drumming became frantic.

Our daughter was released to jump back on the crowded bus. The doors banged behind her. Running up to the open windows, Ted and I promised to write to our family during our 30-day stay in the wilderness.

The bus pulled away. The accountant left. Maybe she trusted us—in this trusting community—or went to put a padlock on our door. This departure had become an absurd theatre piece.

The yellow vehicle crunched down the gravel road. Villagers began to wave and we continued to keep arms up and moving, like dancers on stage. It was a Holden tradition to wave and wave and wave. A lovely ritual, this courtesy resembled a Minnesota good-bye, with one more story to tell, and similar to our Japanese friends who kept waving after we had walked a good block from their home.

Not until the bus went through the shade of the trees by the ice cream shop and curved into the woods, did we stop waving good-bye. Everything seemed flat, with my hiking buddies out of sight. Why had Ted and I signed up for 36 hours a week of hard work, for a month?

Since the bookstore combined post office with general store, that combination was the answer. I bought some stationery to write each hiker personal letters, looked forward to some great correspondence.

Have we ever told our children how Dad and I met, in a parking lot? And my first thought was, *He's a possibility?* How their father, a non-dancer, took Arthur Murray lessons so he could take me to college dances? Then I could describe to our grandchildren how we explored Holden to find solutions to our neighbor problem. Why hadn't we shared these things with them while they were here?

After lunch I watered several baskets of petunias above the loading dock, and saw people assembling for the 1:30 bus. I put down my sprinkling can, walked over to the beat of the drums, and felt like part of this community, doing the ritual. Maybe my brain is hardwired to see God in farewells. Saying goodbye is participation in life together, like singing Happy Birthday to Sara on the coming Sunday. This community is more than Ted and me and our family, but all of the village including the accountant, and the starving world where some don't even have rice. The neighbors, I knew, needed to be included.

Waving the departing villagers off, our farewell community sent them through the shade and around the curve, till the drummers quit. I knew no one on that bus but this time I cried.

Jamila's Rice Pilaf

1 1/2 C brown rice, uncooked
1 C wild rice, uncooked
3/4 C dried cranberries
½ C hazelnuts, chopped
2 green onions, sliced
1 Tab. fresh cilantro (optional)
1 C seasoned rice- wine vinegar

Cook rice (approximately 35 minutes). Mix in the cranberries, hazelnuts, green onion and cilantro. Coat the rice with the rice-wine vinegar.

Hint: The rice vinegar acts as a dressing. The rice and cranberries soak up a lot of the moisture. This dish can be served hot or cold.

Chapter Eight
When Do We Shut Up?

Like wolves and other creatures, the soul and spirit are able to thrive on very little, and sometimes for a long time on nothing.
Clarissa Pinkola Estes

In the woods a mile from the village, a waterfall plunged, dived, bubbled and splashed on Ten-Mile Creek. The name of the creek told us its distance from Lake Chelan. As destination for Sunday afternoon's Meditation Hike, it attracted twenty villagers. Ted wasn't among them; he preferred the carpentry shop.

Our group met at The Ark, a deck on the village green under the bell. The leader Sig explained. "I'll read a poem when we get to the woods. Then we'll be quiet all the way to the falls. OK?"

Crossing the green, walking up the hill past Chalet 14 to the trailhead, we chatted about where we were from and the Sunday chicken dinner just consumed. One woman, who was from Brooklyn, called out to Sig. "When do we shut up?"

Charmed by her question, I squashed my laughter when Sig, a serious young man from South Dakota, said, "In about two minutes, at the sign board."

His poem spoke of listening, looking, touching and smelling whatever the wilderness presented. While he read, I tried to taste the delicate, sweet air. I meditated on breathing and my body's finesse in keeping my lungs pumping. Ted, the mechanical engineer, has said that if God had to take out a patent on the human body, there would be a zillion documents.

Sig asked the Brooklyn woman to lead our group silently while he walked at the end of our line-up. In my treaded-boots once again, I enjoyed the grind and pine-needle aroma of the path. Touching the ragged bark of a giant Douglas Fir, my mind's eye saw attacks by wind, drought, fire, ice, and avalanches. A nearby stump showed its rings for a quick, silent estimate of 100 to 150 years.

This quiet hike differed from being alone. I was aware of the others, receiving non-spoken signals from their pace and body language, as well as from trees and the striped pathfinder plants thriving in the shade. Our silent experience flowed into my hard-wired brain. What would happen if I began to howl like a wolf?

Andrew Newberg describes a haunting saxophone concert in an old church, in his book *Why God Doesn't Go Away?* One man from the audience stood up and bayed like a wild wolf. The author claims that in such a mystical context, baying is acceptable. Other members of the audience must have agreed for they howled, also.

Our woodland opened to areas cleared by every-winter avalanches. A wide swath of sun-loving broad-leafed shrubs prospered in the openness that showed us a valley view with huge piles of copper-tailings from a half-century ago. Tiny alders grew in gravel that covered these mining leftovers, and healed the blight.

The dangers of the wilds became real to me when I crossed a high wooden bridge over a creek, small but filled with boulders. A former medic had told me that a few years ago, a young girl broke both legs when she fell off this bridge. A helicopter had lifted her out for medical care.

My fingers gripped the railing till they hurt. Pausing at the bridge, I made a gap in the middle of our group. No one appeared ahead or behind me. Rounding a corner, I saw a man peeing against the tree trunk. I turned away. "Sorry, wasn't looking."

The embarrassed man pulled himself together, turned back and mumbled, "I thought the group had gone by."

My vow of silence had been broken. After sniffing a Jeffrey pine's vanilla-scented bark, I wanted to nudge someone and caught up with the fast group. But I said nothing. The Brooklyn woman had been right; sometimes we need to shut up.

If I had been there in that old church at the saxophone concert, I might have howled with the others for a liberating unity. Even blue whales, thousands of miles apart sing to each other. Newburg calls the human-wolf-baying a neurological chain of events: "We are not long aloof," he says, "or independent."

The idea of a primal unity grounded me to the path we followed, with the animals who came this way at night, and any other creature that peed in the woods. No one on our meditation hike howled but I believe we felt this unity when we heard the roar of the falls.

Turning a rock-cleft corner, twenty quiet humans approached, practically on tiptoes. A wooden viewing deck brought us over the drop of a 50-foot waterfall. Activated love swept down in the roaring water below us quiet people, and through the tranquil woods. Its steady agitation pounded our ears, and washed over three giant trunks lodged in the bank below. Who had heard them fall, and how long ago was that? Has anyone bounded across the stream on the crazy logjam? And how quickly did that little girl's broken legs heal?

Sig led a prayer for strength and fervor, to survive and protect the earth. No one else spoke. The Brooklyn woman led us back, in comfortable quietness. Not a taut muscle tensed my body which felt naturalized, at one with woods and water. My brain alerted me that it was Sunday and Sara's birthday. I vowed to find her and sing.

But next on my dance card was Lovefest Celebration at the Ark. I went to pick up Ted over at the carpentry shop, where he varnished his CD boxes for the library. Boom-box jazz contrasted with my silent hike. "What's with the music?"

"The younger carpenters all have their favorites. It's going all day." Ted, in his baseball cap and thick glasses, turned off the music and cleaned his paintbrush.

Examining his crafted boxes for the library, I also noticed two big cabinets with "Stan and Ollie" painted on the doors in block letters. "Somebody has a sense of humor," I said, "and there must have been some Stan-and-Ollie moments."

"Nobody admits to that."

"Oh? I've seen a screwdriver notched by an electric shock..."

Ted gave me a don't-remind-me look. He had once received a "memory" plaque from a family member that commemorated an old screwdriver of his that had clashed with electricity-not-turned-off.

I moved on to inspect the well-equipped workspace: chop saw, shaper, drill press, belt sander and more. My father, with two of his brothers, had formed a building-contractor business in the 1920s. I grew up with the squeal of their table saw, and lovely wooden curls from the planer. This place had that same aroma of freshly-cut wood – like Ted's workshop in our barn. He often claimed that when working in the barn, he was always happy.

Ted's fine woodworking provided us with cabinets, tables, chairs and lamps. He and my Dad had built our first house. Inspired by this creative action, my father had confided to us what he liked best about building: "When the batter boards are up, with lines pulled taut, just before the building comes up out of the ground."

There are similarities between these two men, the one I married and the one "who gave me away."

Two, over-six-foot-tall flower "girls" carried baskets for the Lovefest at the Ark. Bedecked with Nordic-horned caps and blonde wigs with pigtails, these two men wore skirts and knee-length ski socks covering most of their muscular, hairy legs. They stood in the wings of The Ark, with baskets of flowers, awaiting their cue.

On the deck, two engaged couples sat regally in chairs draped with billowing, colorful fabrics. Young, beautiful, maybe overwhelmed, they played their part in this exercise of Holden Hilarity. Ted and I didn't know the nearly-wed couples but had heard their stories. Holdenites for a year, they had coincidentally set identical dates in towns a thousand miles apart. So this Lovefest-farewell became one of Holden's absurd celebrations." It began when the big-bruiser "maidens" skipped in, throwing clumps of daisies into a whistling, cat-calling audience.

A guitarist/song-writer began singing about the couples: "John McBride said, "Be by bride" and Sara Eck said, "What the heck." He continued with 24 humorous verses for each pair. Their weddings would be in two weeks, and my brain worked on this two-weeks-from-now information. The date was our golden wedding anniversary.

At open-mike time, the leader encouraged people in the audience: "Come up and say a few words."

A quietness settled in, like a schoolroom when no one knows the answer. "I'm going to mention the closeness of the dates," I whispered to Ted.

"No, don't do it," he said.

The silence stretched. So my soul thrived on very little, and my confidence grew. I bolted to the microphone. "You don't even know me but I have to tell you of a coincidence of wedding dates. Ted and I are here to celebrate our golden wedding and that date is just the same as your weddings. I wish you at least 50 years of happiness."

I didn't add that Ted told me not to say anything. Could they imagine living with the same partner for fifty years, holding different opinions, ideas and goals? My independence, or Ted's reluctance to have me speak, might shock them. I should have told them a time-tested rule is to hold hands when you argue.

These two engaged couples probably would not believe that Ted and I, at that same betrothed jumping-off point, had anything in common with them. Yet Ted had canoed in the Boundary Waters between Minnesota and Canada, and such adventure in his past attracted me to him. Later in our engagement time, our biggest disagreement was over an ash tray.

"Everything in our apartment," I had insisted, "should be special, beautiful, unique – even an ashtray."

"I don't care about such things," he had said.

I yanked my engagement ring off my finger. "The wedding will be called off."

Ted explained his generic ideas about furnishings and why it didn't matter to him that much. I cried a little about my dreams for our first home and then put the ring back on my finger. Ted and I were different and alike, and kept changing. How could I know back then that he would design the perfect house for us a year later?

After the Lovefest, I had just enough time to catch Holden's little bookstore before it closed. Its Post Office window, I noted was closed on Sunday but I expected to find mail for us during the next week.

Besides books, the store sold T-shirts, jackets, sweaters; insulated stainless steel mugs and pencils made from twigs. I wanted to buy stationery to write to my family, and also toothpaste. I asked Rose, a Lodge One neighbor who clerked part-time, "Do you carry toothpaste?"

"Oh, yes, Tom's," she said and pointed to the proper shelf.

Tom's of Maine, Natural Toothpaste with Fluoride flavored with ginger mint, was the only toothpaste there. It's story continued with tiny printing on the box: "No saccharin, no animal products, no preservatives, no dyes...it leaves your mouth with clean, fresh feeling...Try it five times before you can become accustomed to it. Please tell us what you think."

No toothpaste had ever before asked me what I thought of it. I bought Tom's and returned to our room to try it out.

Ted watched, with a skeptical expression, and checked his supply of Crest. "What does it taste like?"

"It doesn't taste like anything." I shook my head. "But I feel proud to use Tom's tooth- paste, and charmed by the fact that Holden only offered one kind. I like the simplicity."

Washing dishes is a simple chore. Ted and I spotted our names on the Dish Team list, following a dinner for 400. Not simple.

Rollicking rock music greeted us as we opened the screen door of the workers' entrance. A tall man in a blue rubberized apron scrubbed pots at a laundry-tray sink. Next to him stood a little girl on a stool. Back in the steamy maze of a huge conveyor-belt dishwasher was a smaller man who sang along with the music and beat out the time with placement of metal lids, baking tins and industrial mixing spoons. "Hi, I'm your captain. What are your names?"

"Ted and Barb." Ted pointed out which was which.

"What's your name?" I asked.

"Yeshua."

Silence. I pondered if his name was a translation of Jesus. He never stopped moving the utensils and cook pots onto the belt, but answered, "Or, you can call me Earl."

Then I remembered the story. I had heard of people calling him Joshua by mistake, Yeshua sometimes went by Earl, probably in his role as Bookstore Manager. Which means that he had ordered the Tom's toothpaste...

Someone had said to Yeshua, about his name: "Your parents had a lot of nerve."

Many Hispanics are named Jesus. Since Yeshua sang and wrote songs for his guitar, maybe he could walk on water, feed the 5000, or at least wash their dishes. I said, "I can call you Yeshua."

"OK, Barb, you help Dale here, and Ted can help me."

Dale, working alongside his daughter, gave me a big rubber spatula to scrape of the food, batter, and baked-on crusts before he dumped the cooking tins in the soapy water. "And don't look in the garbage can," he added, "it's too disgusting."

The steamy atmosphere sucked in whiffs of leftovers, used coffee grounds and orange peals. His daughter giggled. "And smelly!"

The kitchen was divided into clean, and not-clean areas, and meticulously guarded. I was in the not-clean area and felt like an untouchable, an undesirable who lived with a lot of trash around their house. Like the gnome and the witch who had placed piles of junk by our shared easement-roadway. Such ideas floated through my mind and needed to be sorted in the next four weeks.

A heavy industrial-size metal mixing bowl nearly slipped out of my hand into the garbage. Brawny cooks, I imagined, used bowls like this and tossed them aside for us to clean. Couldn't they soak the equipment in water first?

Dale promoted me to a sink for serious scraping with metal spatulas and tuffies. Ted hustled, in the mechanical area with Yeshua, banging equipment down on the moving belt., "We can do it," Yashua rapped. "You're doing good. We're winning."

Two more crew members arrived. The music soared and heavy metal kept a steady beat.

"Wotta team," our captain cried out as hundreds of dishes advanced on us from the first setting. Yeshua never stopped talking, singing, prodding us to keep moving. "We are winning. We'll get you out of here in time for vespers."

That would be 7:00 pm. I planned to go to bed. Today was Sunday, our day off, and this was a far cry from my afternoon meditation hike. Yeshua called a 30-minute break while we waited for dishes from the second-setting. Ted and I sat on the porch steps, exhausted. I quoted drugstore-clerk Rose, a longtime volunteer slightly younger than we were: "Everybody is tired here. Some people call Holden a slave camp."

What would our family say about that? What did we think? When we applied, we didn't pay attention to the extras: Dish Team, Garbology, Bathroom-Cleaning chores. Of course, I didn't have to add on to my day-off schedule, the meditation hike or the afternoon lovefest.

Yeshua's rock beat started again and we moved fast until that last dirty dish ran through the machine. Everything was clean but too-hot-to-touch. Other workers, in the "clean" category, were able to cart the dishes away. We the "Unclean," smelling like dirty dishwater, tidied up our work areas.

"You can mop the floor," Yeshua said to me.

Oh, Yeshua, I said to myself, *I don't mop. Mopping only smears dirt around.*

Yeshua pointed out a large, metal-poled, grey, stringy mass hanging on the wall, and indicated the bucket to be filled. I had heard that he was leaving Holden in a week or so, for a job back east in the music industry. Yeshua might be famous some day. I should mop for him. Besides, Jennifer my boss seemed to like him very much.

I dislodged the mop from the wall but it fell on the floor. I couldn't lift the heavy, disgusting thing. One of the young-men helpers came over. "I'll mop, you fill the bucket."

"Thanks."

I filled the bucket, hung up my apron, and said, "Good night, Captain Yeshua."

Ted wiped down the last of the utility carts, but I didn't wait for him. I not only wanted to shut up, I had to shut down and Tom's toothpaste waited for me. Then I might howl like a wolf.

Dish Team

Clank clink bang boing
wham splash thud crack
and shouts from our captain.
We can do it.

    we fight enemies in holy war
    against crud squashed leftovers
    baked-on peanut butter
    oily smears frantic
    scraping and soaking frenzy
    makes dirty dishes advance.

Clank clink bang boing
wham splash thud crack
our captain counsels:
You're doing good.

    Fast moves to a steady beat
    of heavy metal we in blue
    rubberized uniforms tackle
    giant aluminum bowls to
    steel-wool monster-metal pots.

    Our captain waves them on
    to industrial revolution
    conveyor belts that slide
    inside for torrents of steaming
    sterilizing purifying water.

Clank clink bang boing
wham splash thud crack
oh how our captain sings,
We are winning.
We are winning.

barbara marysdaughter

Chapter Nine
No One Person Can Save The Village

It is your concern when neighbor's wall is on fire. Horace, *Epistle xviii*, 65-8 BCE

A European two-tone alarm filtered through our screened window. Sirens invaded the room to shake us awake. Bare walls ricocheted the insistent scream. We absorbed, inhaled, tasted its cry of danger. Our little clock showed only 9:00 PM, for we had gone to bed early.

A woman's voice exploded from the village PA system with "first response team" and "go to main hose-house." Neighbors ran down the hallway. In our pajamas, Ted and I looked out the window at people who walked in military style on Holden's main road, toward a building that housed the wailing electronic communications.

For months an out-of-control brushfire had raged across the lake from Holden. Rangers said it would never jump over the lake. But could it spread some other way? Ted sniffed the air by our window. "No smoke in the air."

Gifted with a talent for spotting smoke on a distant horizon or smelling it in the tiniest breeze, Ted knows about fire. When he was 17, his father died in a cabin fire while on a fishing trip in California. At the funeral, Ted's older brother had lifted the lid of the closed coffin to see the father's body "burned beyond recognition." Ted doesn't like to talk about it. The horror of such a death by fire never goes away.

The pine trunk still grew close to our second-floor window. Could we shimmy down that, if necessary, or would flames shoot up, at us? Could we get the screen off? "Shouldn't we get out of here?"

Ted took his jacket out of the closet.

My mouth went dry. "What should I take with me? My purse?"

Would someone pound on our door when it was time to go? Upstairs in an ancient wooden barracks, we had counted on newly installed sprinklers and a super-sensitive smoke alarm. This loud, well-articulated voice on the PA system sent a new message: "All clear. All clear."

I collapsed on Ted's bed. "Do you think we should go back to sleep?"

Ted gave me a weary look. "You want me to go around with a fireman's axe, breaking down burning doors and rescuing fair damsels?"

We turned out the lights. But that same wailing siren, feminine voice, and running-steps outside our door awakened us again at midnight. This time Ted opened our door to the hallway. A young neighbor crouched there, tying his boot strings.

"Should we evacuate?" I asked the neighbor.

"Naw. Not yet. It's probably another false alarm. The smoke devices are sensitive. A hot shower triggers the system." He stood up and left the building.

Somebody's shower was stealing our much-needed rest. Val, the village medic who lived next door, had told me on that first day – after I came out of the men's bathroom – to switch on the fan before showering. I willed myself again, never to forget.

Weary from my obligations, I noticed that down the hallway, the washing machine door stood open at last. After checking all day with no luck, I decided to start a load. Ted, in his extreme tiredness and contemplation of cement-finishing work the next day, sank back onto his bed.

How could we volunteers accomplish everything we needed to do? After all, this month of service at Holden represented our fiftieth-anniversary celebration. Here voluntarily, quite literally, we had to get our rest to stay healthy. Nevertheless, some kind of determination assured me that we would not leave before our month-long contract was up on September 1. We would begin soon to tell new friends about our harassment, Ted's arrest, and gather opinions, suggestions in our hope to solve the problem.

On the bulletin board in the dining hall, a list of rules against such frivolities as washing clothes at midnight called out to me. I should have known. But I hadn't heard the thumping of my wash or thought of neighbors close to the noise. Even the use of water during a fire, I suddenly realized, could be a felony.

What if our troublesome neighbor's house was on fire? Would we risk our lives to save it? Rescue unlovable neighbors? Do we know what we'll do in an emergency? Couldn't hurt to explore the depths of that question, the next time I had a few moments. And I needed to read a new book which sounded helpful: *The Sociopath Next Door* by Martha Stout.

According to a review, the author is a clinical instructor of psychiatry at Harvard Medical School. She defines sociopath as one lacking a conscience. That fits our neighbors. Dr. Stout describes sociopaths as exceptionally good at lying: another direct hit. Most astounding: sociopaths represent four percent of our population, or one in 25 people.

That kind of information made me feel less alone. Perhaps, those of us who are targets can help each other. We could educate deputies, police officers and judges to deal with sociopaths who (according to Dr. Stout's book) "live to dominate and are thrilled to win."

The Gnome and the Witch, have never made it clear what we have done to earn their hatred. They made up complaints about us driving fast, back and forth on the easement, stealing tools from their shed, running over their dog and poisoning their mule. We surmise they want us to disappear so they can use some of our land. It's the not-knowing that keeps my body ever-tense, in a warrior state, vengeful, humiliated and wanting to lash back.

With the lawn sprinkler set, by Lodge One first thing, I was ready for the 6:00 am garden briefing from Jennifer: seed the lawn, spread compost, and weed. I tried to remember that work is a form of prayer leading to solved-problems, and gardening cooperates with creation itself. Perhaps my workday with the earth can form a bridge with this sociopath I call a witch, who works back in California as a gardener.

Our gardening crew of five walked out of the dining hall together. Jennifer said gently, "And Barbara, a resident of Lodge One complained about water on porch steps, and mud on the swing."

Oh, oh. Someone does keep track of my goofs. Does that person know how heavy my filled watering can is? And how difficult to direct its spout accurately? Is the complainer's room next to the washing machine?

Early-assembling kitchen crew reminded me that I had not sung for Sara yet. A pretty, young woman with brown hair pushed back from her face, tied a bow in her apron strings, and picked up a kitchen knife. I asked, "Are you Sara?

She looked surprised and stopped her gathering of onions on the chopping block.

"Was your birthday Sunday?" I continued.

"How did you know?"

Explaining how her mother took a photo of my family, and confided to me about missing Sara's birthday, I apologized about being one-day late. Singing a quick version, maybe off-key, I asked, "How did you celebrate?"

"No one knew." She chopped that first onion faster.

My face must have revealed concern. Sara said, "I'm going home next week."

"Say hello to your mother."

My Shi-bashi movements on the ice cream deck at 6:45 am called to me. Sara went along, inside my head. She didn't seem to fit in here, either, and made me think of Lauren and Nathan, and how our grandchildren didn't feel comfortable at Holden.

Our leader, Dianne, gave us the history of the exercise-meditation form: "More ancient than yoga or tai chi, Shi-bashi fell out of favor, for centuries. Several years ago Filipina Christians saw it as a meditation reflecting their Asian backgrounds, and settled on these 18 movements."

Our group of seven formed a circle. Dianne continued: "I like the movements because they occupy my mind and keep me from making those mental to-do lists." Knowingly, most of us nodded and chuckled.

In a quiet voice, Dianne led us in the Morning Vocation Prayer. Our leader suggested we close our eyes. Her instructions told us to breathe deeply, place hands on navel, and bring feet together. Her meditative words guided us: "I return to the place I was born."

An image of my thirty-four-year-old mother popped onto my inner screen. I saw a younger image, than I could possibly remember, of my pregnant mother entering Christian Hospital in North St. Louis. It is snowing, which is unusual for May in Missouri.

Dianne continued: "I am born." She told us to open eyes, arms and legs wide, and make a "gentle smile." I thought of Sara being born and her mother singing to her.

My snapped-open eyes took in surrounding pine trees with limbs that reached toward a clear sky. The snow on our highest peaks seemed appropriate, as did the energy that radiated from the group. Our leader told us to hold our hands above our head and "move them down in front of our bellies." The men and women in our circle complied and the prayer continued: "I carve a place for myself in the world."

My head spun with the 77 places I have carved for myself from student to wife to mother to cook to writer to teacher to gardener, and more. On my mind screen, I saw my hiking buddies, children and grandchildren posing for a group picture, with our new title: *The Trench Foot Gapsters*, which they had chalked on the sidewalk.

The image melded into a sisterbrothersister/brothersister/mother/ grandmother religious medal, a heritage medallion. That reminded me to ask my daily question at the post office, after class: "Anything for Johnsons?"

"No-o-o-o." The young woman who worked there showed great compassion about our lack of mail. She looked as sorry as I felt.

Another night of false alarms convinced Ted and me that no matter how tired we were, we had to learn fire procedures. Tom, Holden's Fire Chief, chaired the Fire-Hose Session scheduled for late afternoon.

A young man of slight build, Tom walked with military bearing into the Creekside meeting room. He had pale skin and, as usual, wore a red bandana on his head. Usually laughing, he joked about our large group gathered together.

"After a night of fire alarms, villagers get real interested in fire prevention. Everyone should take safety seriously in this environment. When you hear the siren, take a deep breath, don't panic, remember that no one person can save the village. Calm down, don't run. You might trip. There will be about 70 people responding."

He told us about the Chalet-Two fire ten years earlier: "It only took one hour before the whole house collapsed. Nothing could be done. The chalets still don't have sprinkler systems."

Tom showed us the two types of fire extinguishers installed in every building in the village.

"Where is the one closest to where you sleep?" he asked.

"Where?" I whispered to Ted.

"I've seen it. Either on the porch or in the back hall."

Others in the class conducted similar conversations. The fire Chief had our attention. He demonstrated how each of the extinguishers worked. They called for strength, good timing. I felt inadequate.

Tom showed a film of brushfire fighters, familiar subject to Ted and me for we had been through three such fires in Los Angeles. One had started in the Santa Susanna mountains behind our house and we had called it in. That brushfire raced 20 miles to the ocean at Malibu.

Our next house, on the slope of these mountains, presented itself as first in line when the firestorm came over the mountains from Simi Valley. That storm looked like a red blizzard pouring over our tile roof, watered-down wood-deck, and onto my fire-fighting husband and son. Ted and Matt wore their armor of bicycle helmets, wet towels, heavy jackets and boots.

I had been inside with our dog and cat, and bathtub full of water. That was on our prep list of things to do in case of fire. When I saw the red "flakes" descend upon Ted and Matt, I thought we had made a mistake to stay. Yet our house endured and so did we, to fight with more confidence, a similar firestorm years later.

"Now that you've had this class," Tom announced, "you are expected to respond to the alarm. Let's look at the main callboard."

We walked down the hall to the Electronic Simplex board where he demonstrated the flashing lights when an alarm is pulled. He showed us the microphone:

"Several women in the village are fast about getting here, and good at announcing. They tell the First Response Team to go to the site of the alarm. The rest of you go to the fire hose storage shed she designates. Line up, count off a team of 20. The rest can leave. First person in line is captain."

Captain? I didn't want to be Captain even with my experience handling hoses. I shrank to the back of the class. Tom said the second in line is in charge of the Y-valve that allows two hoses to hook up. He emphasized strength to handle hoses when the water is turned on. "Don't take out hoses unless First Response Team tells you, because the hoses are tough to put back."

Maybe I could handle the Y-valve. I recalled that euphoric three-in-the-morning feeling of accomplishment after the firestorm had swept by our house and all was safe. On the deck, talking to the fire-fighters who had finally made it up to our site, we basked in that glow of success against a formidable force.

That was a beautiful October morning for us. The firemen praised our work but others still fought for their lives and homes, down below and beyond the next ridge of mountains. The firemen gave us a regulation fire hose that connected to the hydrant at the edge of our yard, for that inevitable next fire.

At Holden the fire alarm went off the next morning during the final movements of Shi-bashi. Mustn't run, I told myself. Besides, I didn't want to get there first and be Captain. My fellow meditators ignored the intrusive sound. They probably had not attended Tom's fire-hose session, and had no commitment.

I dawdled. Why disrupt our beautiful meditation? Who would know if I didn't go? The wailing alert wafted over the rooftop of Village Center to dent my ear drums. A woman's voice, clearer and more understandable than ever before, advised, "Proceed to lower Chalet hose house."

That was across the street from our meditation circle. No longer concentrating on Shi-bashi, I noticed my right foot starting to turn toward the steps of the deck. One more wail, plus instruction, and I started down the six wooden steps. I whispered, "Have to go."

The woman's voice from the electronic board: "All clear, all clear."

Rejoining our circle in time for the final bowing to each member, I brought my hands together in front of my face to whisper Namaste, a spiritual recognition of members of our group. I felt safe. For the next alarm, I decided to walk to the hose house, be captain or Y-valve steward as part of the more-than-one-person group saving the village.

At dinner, Fire Chief Tom (who told me he has no connection with Tom's toothpaste) sat next to Ted at our round table. Tom said he had never before done any fire-fighting but learned it on the job this past year at Holden.

Ted explained about our fire adventures on the edge of the San Fernando Valley. Tom laughed. "You have more experience than I do."

The next day in Shi-bashi, I returned to the place where I was born, moved along in my meditation to concerns in the hallway of Lodge One. There my laundry had throbbed noisily at midnight, then my sprinkling can dribbled on the porch furniture, my shoes left mud on the floor. My meditative state traveled onward to home, and our neighbor's place, all afire.

Alienated Sociopaths:

(from American Psychiatric Assn.)

– won't get along with neighbors. Most will believe they are justified in this because they feel they were cheated in some way themselves, by society.

Chapter Ten
Holy Hot Hilarity

One could do worse than being a swinger of birches.
Robert Frost

"It's the sauna tonight," I said. With swimsuits and towels, Ted and I walked to the city-sauna, across the sidewalk from the dining hall. That's as *downtown* as you get in Holden Village. Cord wood piled up on the porch near its outside-access to the firebox. We both looked up at the cabin's chimney but there was no smoke coming out.

"Maybe there's danger of sparks so close to the old hotel," I suggested.

Ted shook his head: "I don't think the sauna's been stoked."

I aimed my elbow at his ribcage, and jabbed. "Maybe you haven't been stoked."

He pulled open the heavy, carved door. We entered the wind-catcher ante-room. Here stoic sauna enthusiasts shift from daily routine to ephemeral reflections, visions and good conversations. A welcoming wooden bench beckoned us to remove our shoes. Wall pegs waited for clothing. The cold dip, a built-in square tub, overflowed with fresh, icy water into a moat-like drain.

History shows the sauna is more ancient than Roman steam baths. Finnish sauna began in Siberia with Finno-Hungarian peoples; references appear in the Finnish epic *Kalevala*, a traditional poetic song:

Come now, God, into the vapor, father of the sky,
into the warmth so as to bring about health…
Water on those hot stones, may it be changed to honey…
Let a river of honey flow, let a pond of honey seep through to ooze…
seep through the pile of stones, through the moss-caulked sauna.

Fellow villager Mark Kremen-Teo, a Native American volunteering at Holden for 18 years, sees similarities in sauna culture with his sweat-lodge tradition: "It takes three hours to heat the lodge to 140-160 degrees."

The grey-bearded man, who told me he was just as old as I was, added, "We throw water on granite grandfather-stones which are thousands of years old and three-feet in diameter. When the hot stones glow, we move them with deer antlers."

At a Chumash Native-American Long Dance Ceremony in San Luis Obispo County, I told him, I had once felt this holy, spiritual connection with historic grandmothers. Mark added, "The steam represents the grandfathers coming back to take away impurities in our bodies."

Here in the ante-room where Ted and I stood, Finns often threw after-sauna parties with special food and strong drink. Guests, assuming there will be another party soon, save their thank-you's for that next occasion, greeting hosts with, "Thank you for the last party."

Ted opened the door into the main sauna room. Heat slapped our faces. Smoke or not, it was stoked. Mirage-like heat waves distorted the three tiers of wooden benches. Dim lighting forced us to squint through heat waves to search out the benches for others in the sauna. But no one baked in the pulsating, scorching heat.

We quickly changed into our swimsuits, put clothing on pegs and stepped barefoot onto hot wooden-slat floor, to lie on the lowest bench.

"Higher is hotter," Ted recalled.

Spreading large "Hot Hilarity" towels purchased at Holden years before, we settled on our backs. Feet propped against opposite walls; heads touched. Our symmetrical pose soothed some artistic or mystical need of mine. Could I receive important vibes this way from a husband who doesn't like to stir up his feelings? Could we live more deeply?

Finns talk about heat quality in their sauna the way the French talk about wine. According to a manual written by Howard Hong, long-time villager, Holden's sauna temperature reaches 185-210 F, enough to hard-boil an egg. So, would our eyes turn into Easter eggs? Could we endure the heat as we melted onto the benches, draped like Dali's limp watches hanging on tree limbs? Directions on the sauna door advised 20-30 minutes for us to sweat; then cool off in ante-room before the plunge, and repeat. A complete sauna takes an hour.

Naked people in a sauna are not shocking, proclaims Astrid, quoted in Hong's book: "To have a sauna bath without clothes is much different from having one in a bathing suit which causes perspiration and skin infections. The sauna is a holy place, and you just don't have any sinful thoughts."

OK, I asked myself, is the sauna holier than a church or synagogue? Or the great outdoors? Fifteen years earlier Ted and I tried Holden's historic creek-side sauna. Heated up to our limit, we had jumped into a streamed of melted-snow, rushing over small boulders. That leap of faith shocked every fiber of life in us but achieved a certain holiness in our memories.

These qualities of sinfulness and holiness differ in our individual definitions. For example, is a courtroom a place where justice prevails with a holiness of the law? In Laura Blumenfeld's book, *Revenge*, the lawyer/writer says "all are not equal in court, and decisions can be horrible."

Her words surprised me. At the same time, her book recalled the time when Ted and I spent three years attempting legal efforts to stop our neighbors' harassment. At the first hearing, we found frustration. The Gnome intimidated the judge with his blustering presence so much that the judge called in another bailiff to help maintain order.

But Ted and I were never called on to speak. Like Dante's inferno, life became "...one great furnace flam'd, yet from those flames no light... but torture without end." That succinctly sums up our futile legal experience.

Still, it's another topic to examine while in the sauna, along with questions about sex. Studies report that most people think about sex every few seconds, even old geezers and crones married for fifty years.

The dry heat of the sauna enveloped my body. Its welcoming intensity seeped into pores, dried out sinuses. "Ted, are you sweating yet?"

"No, I think I'll move up a level. Want to go with me?"

I blew on my arm. "This pastor from upstate said that in the sauna if your breath feels hot, it's time to move out." I stretched up to his level and blew on his arm.

"There's no difference between the air in here and your breath."

"Is that a compliment?"

"Just stay till you sweat."

"That gives us time to think."

"About what?" Ted turned over and re-arranged his towel.

Instead of "sinful thoughts," I quoted the sauna expert: "This guy said that the early Finnish sauna called for a fire in the middle of a room without a chimney. When it burned out and smoke disappeared, that's when people came in. They called it a *sava*, which means smoke in Finnish."

Ted didn't answer. Sometimes we seem to be the classic opposites attracted to each other. But discord may be normal and goes back to ancient biology when we were all single cells and ate each other. So our heritage is cannibalism and selfishness, with genes focused on survival. All of that explains the first murder, battle, war, ruthless corporation, divorce, and diverse differences of opinion. How are we to change traits written in our genetic code? And how can we remember to thank our host for the "last time"?

The fire crackled and metal stove expanded with little *tings* that quieted my body and mind. With no piped-in music, just the heat that sizzles our chromosomes, the sauna summons out what we shall be, and discerns the spirit of our beloved. What if we fall asleep and dry out like a couple of apricots?

Ted sat up. "I'm sweating all over, right now."

Couldn't be 20 minutes, but who had a wristwatch? Entering the wind-catcher room, we both gulped normal air, contemplated the cold plunge in front of us but agreed to shower in our lodge. We could think whatever sinful thoughts occurred to us.

A friend from Switzerland, a champion of the sauna, told me she had loved the experience from the first one she ever tried – not in Finland, nor even in Europe. Her first sauna was in Los Angeles. "I'm always cold," Verena had said, "and at last I could get warm."

In her home on California's central coast, she installed an electric-powered sauna which warms slowly. "If I go in when it's just heating up, I warm up gradually, too, and can stay longer. Thirty minutes." She smiled at the thought and added, "And never plunge to cool off."

Now recovered from broken collarbone and ribs (bicycle accident), Verena added, "The sauna healed me in less than six weeks. The heat is relaxing and it emptied my mind."

Smoke spiraled out of the sauna chimney the next day and I inhaled the woody scent. My shoulders relaxed, dropped away from my ears when I walked by the sauna hut after work. This will be a daily ritual, I planned, like the Finnish athletes who won't go on the road without their portable saunas.

Racing to our lodge to change into my suit, I recalled that the manual advised: "Hurry is the worst enemy of sauna." Forty-five minutes remained before dinner. Ted worked late on the cement finishing so I left him a note. He had once been enthusiastic about the sauna but didn't want visitations into his impurities, meditations, deep discussions or sharing of thoughts. He was not going to ask for help with our neighbor problem at Holden, not in the sauna or elsewhere. After those three hours in the County Jail, he probably couldn't face continued reminders of the neighbors' vendetta.

We had both agreed on no more lawyers because our extra cushion of savings had been flattened by the courts. Options included county agencies and/or installation of a cam recorder in our car to document events. Constant surveillance and documentation blotted out any kind of life I wanted to live.

That afternoon when I stepped into the sauna, I met Carrie, a fifty-ish blonde cooling off in the ante-room. "I have my priorities in the right place," she said with a laugh. "Just got off the afternoon bus and headed here first."

"Great." I shook her hand. "So I'm not the only fan."

"Oh, no. Just wait till about midnight. My husband and a lot of the others will be here."

"Is that when the interesting discussions go on?"

"Since the beginning of Holden," she assured me. "We've been here in the winter and the sauna benches are full of people discussing everything from Martin Luther and fellow monks spending all their money on beer, to the whole idea that Christianity is not an old-lady society."

Ignoring the swipe at us old ladies, I asked about winter in the village. "Have you been here when the snow was deep?"

"Oh, yes." Carrie began to gather her belongings. "The funniest thing was when we dashed from chalet to sauna in bathing suit, towel and snow shoes."

Carrie opened the heavy outer door to leave and I stepped into the empty heat-room. Trustingly, I submitted to the sauna following Astrid's advice in the manual: "It's like weekly confession, where you leave burdens of the week and find the wholeness of the human being."

Burdens of those three years of harassment welled up within me. Calming heat led me away into other events and people I've encountered. My mind went where it pleased. I watched it go to an old bumper sticker saying *Being a better neighbor makes all neighbors better.*

Widening that concept for universal concerns and world politics, seemed easier to me than dealing with the two irrational people we have to drive by every day at home. At first Ted and I had been good neighbors by sharing meals, garden produce, and chit chat with this newly-moved-in family. Something changed after we had finished building our house.

They became a gnome and witch, instructing their teen-aged son: "Cuss them out. The Johnsons need it."

In my sauna stupor, I re-ran how these experienced con-artists set us up, put out a contract on us. My pursuit of being a better neighbor seemed infinite, unending as I roasted on the second-level bench.

One of the male Japanese volunteers, Reishi, came in and settled on the third-level. The shy, strong jawed, polite college student nodded to me, and I nodded back. Soon I forgot he was there and, like Carrie in the sauna, I considered my priorities. Sauna, Shi-bashi and working out the neighbor problem lined up along with the necessities of laundry, gardening and extras like Dish Team and Garbology, afternoon ice cream, and piano practicing.

My jazz and boogie-woogie book waited in my duffel. What I needed was a secluded piano where I wouldn't bother anyone who listened to my stumbling, beginner-type playing. After a 40-year hiatus from piano lessons and practice, my renewed interest seems a miracle. As a pre-teen, I had argued with my parents about not practicing. Now my sheet music comes with me on trips, along with high hopes of finding a piano to use.

The best piano location for me at Holden was the schoolhouse, empty by mid-afternoon and across the street from the ice cream shop. Following my end-of-workday sauna and shower, I put on a favorite, long, loose-flowing dress and walked to the schoolhouse. My plans called for playing every piece in my music book. Favorites were *Worried Man Blues* (with title changed to *Worried Woman Blues*), *Lonesome Road* (which I hoped to memorize), and *St. James Infirmary Blues*. My music ranked high among priorities.

Ted arrived at the schoolhouse directly from work, with dried cement decorating his jeans, shoulders slumped, body looking eager for a break. I closed my music book. We strolled together across the street to pick out the flavor of the day. Like on a date, this delightful ritual played out on the shady deck. We tongued the sweetness of ice cream and talked about things like cement finishing.

"Everyone pitches in," Ted explained, "the electricians, plumbers and Mavericks. Practically every one in the operations department. When that concrete mixer comes down the street, we have to move."

"A concrete mixer? Here at Holden?" I had been working on the new lawn areas and missed it all. "I thought they'd use something like the big mixing equipment from the kitchen." Ted gave me a weary look. "Holden has its own concrete truck. Came on a barge years ago. They keep it in that garage with all the old school buses."

His tiredness stole the enjoyment from our interlude. Ted didn't finish his ice cream cone. And the job, a new patio in front of the big meeting building, wasn't finished either The next day promised even harder work. His weariness begged for the sauna.

Not everyone is a sauna fan. "CJ," a Holden volunteer in the laundry, believed it made one's skin tough. She based that upon her experience as a nurse with Finns in a northern Minnesota nursing home. A large number of them did sauna, by wheelchair, every Saturday night.

Astonished, I imagined wheelchairs maneuvering up the stairs to the high benches. And what about sizzling metal armrests and footholds? But CJ continued: "The old people carried evergreen branches, soaked in water to freshen them, for whisking their backs. Something – maybe the sauna, maybe the whisking – made their skin like elephant's hide. I couldn't penetrate one woman's skin when I had to give her a shot."

I wanted to know if they were helped out of the wheelchairs and onto the low benches? What were they wearing? Did they take out hostilities in whisking each others' backs with those evergreen branches? Was it a holy experience? But CJ had to go back to her laundry work. She recommended a Garrison Keillor song, *The Finn Who Would Not Take a Sauna.*

A 16-versed saga, it tells about a young man "sensitive to temperature change," in love with a woman who refuses to marry a man who will not take a sauna. The couple goes out to the sauna shack anyway, takes off their clothes and – here are some lyrics;

She steamed him and she boiled him until his skin turned red
She poured it on until his brains were boiling in his head.
To increase his circulation, and to soften up his hide
She cut a couple birch boughs, and beat him till he cried.

Four verses later, he dashes down to the frozen lake, leaps through the chopped-out hole, and then remembers, "I can't swim!" His lady-love fishes him out and they get married that night.

Milder and safer than that song were the rules in the Hong manual: *Never rush from heat to cold. Whisk your back, or another person's back if asked to do so. A good outlet for hidden hostility. Custom demands people in a sauna wash each other's back when asked. At the end, cool off, relax, dry yourself till you've stopped sweating; take a 10-minute rest.*

When I finished my 40-minute sauna of quiet peace, I nodded to the Japanese young man, who looked relaxed and at ease. He had not suggested I wash or whisk his back. But I knew small birch trees grew near the Ten-Mile Waterfall trail, and planned to cut some. Humming the Keillor song, I considered whisking Ted till he cried while his brains boiled in his head.

On my way out of the sauna hut, I read the carving on the door, an artistic flowing of symbols and words:: *Walk through porticos giving thanks… Claim Yahweh, all the earth.* I read wood-box signs, too: *No scraps; kindling only. Take caution: wood may have nails. Have a fantastic time sweating your brains out.*

The sauna remained closed for the rest of our dry, crisp summer because of the high fire hazard of dry brush. Across the lake, the brush fire continued to consume the chaparral. Air we breathed seemed hot like in the sauna and drinking water became an obsession. Our bodies felt dry and brittle. Even the chain-saw gang who cut up firewood for the Holden winter curtailed their spark-throwing work. They sawed in the dewy morning or damp night air.

The three birch-tree boughs I had collected found their way back, in my arms, to their woods. Those sauna signs spoke to me and I watched out for splinters, retrieved brains during any kind of cool down, and claimed the universe. Difficult neighbors might ask, sometime, for whisking or washing of their backs.

Surely, I wanted to believe, I would comply.

The Crowned Prince Of Minnesota

My husband's hometown clings to a curve
in a Minnesota lake that is seventeenth
largest out of ten thousand. Its treasures
include lakeside ballroom and band shell.

A screened-porch at Ted's family home
in Glenwood leads to shore where rowboat
once awaited his transformation of it
into sailboat with sideboards.

Glenwood's main street glides up from lake
past Lutheran church to glacier-scraped valley.
A Catholic steeple pokes out of trees
closer to lakeshore.

Wall-eyed pike attract fishing crowds in summer.
Badgers swim near shore before dawn loons call
and winter dots frozen lake with fishing houses.

Ski-jump hill splats boys like Ted on breakneck slope.
This was home for a kid who built an ice boat,
stitched its sails on his mother's sewing machine.

A baby caboose born
when brother and sister were in their twenties
Ted reveled in only-child splendor.
I call him the Crowned Prince of Minnesota

Royally engaged I had visited, with my parents
from Missouri to meet his mother, aunt Mathilda
sister Doris , uncle Bob, cousin Dorothy newly
engaged to school principal Arne Petersen.
We curtsied to cousins on farms, ate lefse and
fuddyman, drove to terrace mill where Ted's
grandparents lie in the churchyard.

After brassy band music by lakeside we sauntered
over to dairy queen where I fell in love with
the hometown of my crowned prince.

barbara marysdaughter

Chapter Eleven
To Tolerate the Intolerant

Even if they are a crowd of sorrows who violently sweep your house empty of its furniture, still, treat each guest honorably. Rumi _

When breakfast announcements ended, Dianne asked me to read my glacier poem. Once I started I could tell the quiet audience was listening. Afterwards several people spoke to me. Among them was Karen, from Seattle, who had just climbed Spider Glacier with a group: "It was great and I had never been backpacking before. Our leaders checked everything out the week before. We knew what to expect."

She made it sound easy and from then on we greeted each other as *Glacier Climber*.

Holden's school bus delivered more new villagers in time for lunch. A smiling young man, with kind eyes, took the last seat at our round table for eight. I categorized him, with his clipped beard and moustache, plaid shirt and jeans, as a generic type here at the village, probably in his forties. He looked directly at us, dressed in our jeans, old plaid shirts and work boots. Ted still wore his billed cap, lightly covered with sawdust. My mud-splattered sun hat hid under the chair. The newcomer caught my eye: "I think I know you."

Being a generic type myself with short gray hair, a few wrinkles but still able to climb a glacier, I wasn't surprised. Serious about this, he continued, "Where do you live?"

"San Luis Obispo County."

That didn't help but he wouldn't give up.

"We lived in Los Angeles before that."

His eyes gleamed. "What part of L.A.?"

"San Fernando Valley."

He smiled. "Keep going."

"Chatsworth."

He shouted out the name of a church where Ted and I had been active for 35 years. "Holy Shepherd." I felt cold shivers. Holden's boisterous mealtimes brought forth our past life. He remembered our house and school-age children thirty years ago. His name was Ron LaPeta, and we knew the name. I wanted to tell him I was now a glacier climber.

At Holden everyone builds on each other. The cooks claim their food "stirs up passion." All of us at Ron's table continued talking and slurping our well-seasoned soup, passing the fresh bread and salad around, and picking up on Ron's life. A pastor in Washington state, he explained that his family sat at other tables, wherever there was room. His wife Cynthia taught theology and was presenting a series on loving one's neighbor.

Passionate and alert about that subject, I felt obsessed to be in her class. Reflections on our troublesome neighbors whirled around my brain to slop over into this remote place that teaches empathy in the wilderness. Healing thoughts sank into my brain. I wouldn't stall, or rant and cry about getting even, or wish for a cosmic Mafia to help me out. Lessons on loving my neighbor may show me the way.

Outside the dining hall, Ron introduced me to the warm and intensely-focused Cynthia. Energy erupted from the couple. I put off my return to sprinkling and weeding to dally, and talk with them about their two teen-aged sons, life in Washington state, and I promised to attend Cynthia's first class. I would take time off in my role of perpetual student: "I'll be there."

That afternoon I transplanted daisies, working with a new fellow gardener, Nancy Johnson from Minneapolis, younger than me by twenty years and vice president of an investment firm. Her efficiency bubbled over into our gardening chores. The short, sturdy, confident woman told me, "Marve and I come here every year with friends from our church."

I told her that our middle child had the same name, and that was a good start.

"My husband Marve is already having coffee with your husband." The trim young woman pointed to the two men seated on a bench by the Sauna Hut. I felt good that Ted had a buddy.

Nancy, a strong and efficient gardener, arrived with her own Stanley clipper, a compact tool that folds up into a case the size of a deck of cards. Like a Swiss army knife, the Stanley becomes a saw, lopper, scissors or anything you need in gardening. Or life.

Enjoying camaraderie like our husbands, we severed daisy roots with our shovels. The smell of rich loamy dirt rose in the air. It seemed cruel to move large sections of the flourishing flowers, but this stand needed space. Like all of us at times.

In Lodge Four's side garden, we gave the newcomers compost, and water. Nancy used her Stanley to chop off blooms in a life-giving act. Maybe good health called for brutality, a crowd of sorrows, like Ted's arrest. Where does that painful page in our history lead us?.

Cynthia's first class brought more realities to me, with her basic questions: "What is going on? What is the alternative? What ought to be?"

She gave us leeway for uncertainties. H. L. Mencken had said, "Truly civilized people are always skeptical and tolerant...their culture based on *I am not too sure*."

Scrawling some notes, I tried to keep up with this dynamo of a woman. Short, small-boned and skinny as a kid, she wore jeans. Her light-brown hair puffed-out in a page boy. She moved like a dancer, or gymnast with that graceful curved spine as she threw her arms out to address the thirty or more of us in the Fireside Room.

We sat on wooden "library" chairs from mining days, updated with cushions. Some class members stretched out on the balcony floor, to peek over the edge. Cynthia let us hear her brain work, fast as a computer. She changed her mind, encouraged dialogue, drew in the timid. We considered love-your-neighbor-as-yourself from this viewpoint: we often don't love ourselves.

Her challenge made me ponder. What if loving ourselves is the element upsetting a dis-gruntled, accomplished jungle fighter using his skills against us? Ted and I love our lives, our-selves, and don't want to change that. We want to have fun in a hundred million different ways. Cynthia's class is one of those ways: serious fun for me. Here I may see that our self-love is what ticks off this sociopath, full-pensioned veteran that we must drive by each day.

When I was younger, I thrashed out such ideas in small groups. The command to love our enemy or neighbor – an idea I supported – lost out in these discussions, in favor of urgent self-defense. Smugly, I would answer, "No one has ever tried loving their enemies. It might work."

Working meant changing – starting with ourselves. That sounded like solid, radical theology to me. The word *neighbors* included everyone, the good and bad, and that's the sticky point. Can we love terrorists who kill themselves along with their victims? Is it a virtue to despise only what they do?

Sunday night before one of Cynthia's final sessions on neighborly life, Ted and I sat out on our porch with neighbors from our 50-room lodge. We wanted to get to know them.

We non-smokers rarely used the second-floor porch, a designated smoking spot with its faint, stale-tobacco smell. Holden tolerates addictions people have with this subtle acceptance, which may influence some to quit.

This evening at the end of the porch, 20 feet away from our group, there was only one smoker. Reishi, a Japanese volunteer, sat near the ash tray to light up. His usual stoic expression emphasized his high cheekbones. Confident, he also appeared unassuming, a non-combatant.

Village life spread out below our porch. We faced the dining hall hubbub of the second setting of dinner, families pouring in the back and front door. Across the village's main street, old mining buildings, transformed into modern lodges with porches and hanging baskets of petunias, stood at the foot of snow-covered peaks soaring as high as 9000 feet.

Settled into relaxing post-dinner positions, feet up, heads propped by cushions, our group spoke in pleasantries. One of the young women who taught the Narnia children's class, used the word *Japs*. Reishi at the other end of our porch jerked his head, and gave us a blank look. The woman, with pulled-back ponytail, used the word again. I whispered, "We shouldn't say that."

No one seemed to hear my little-girl's voice which may only send one message: "I don't want to cause trouble." Partly true, as a new member of the community, and older as in "not with it," I became inconsequential. The group, and I was obviously not part of it, found my comment irrelevant. A younger woman, under a hanging basket of flowers I had watered that morning, launched a story about her grandfather, quoting him in a loud voice, "I don't trust Japs."

Reishi snubbed his cigarette, looked up with a blank expression, and strode toward the door. Did he mumble something as he left? A spiral of smoke rose to the porch ceiling.

Rose, a longtime volunteer in her sixties and from a nearby small town, changed the subject slightly. "The Mexicans are taking over our town. Everything in the stores is in Spanish. The Mexicans had the nerve to sing the National Anthem in Spanish on the Fourth of July."

Isn't that better than singing the Mexican anthem? That question remained in my head. I decided to give the group facts from our daughter Judy's experiences in Half Moon Bay, California where half of the population speaks Spanish: "Most Spanish-speaking workers desperately want to learn English but have little time or energy after a day in the fields, and no extra money for classes."

Although I spoke louder this time, they ignored my comment. The general topic gained momentum. Another woman in the swing, Ethel, who had told me she had had a tough life, pointed out how the Jews had taken over the world. Ted, who sat near the door to our hallway, turned his face from the group, bent over and rushed for the door. He escaped.

In the opposite corner, I was trapped and defeated. Ethel must have felt my discomfort for she conceded, "There has to be room on earth for all people."

At Holden everyone is an immigrant who came from somewhere else, starting with the miners. What else can we be but immigrants? Was her comment another way to say: *Go back where you came from? All of us?*

Down below on the street, several men walked by dressed in kilts, ultra-burly military-grade camouflage cloth, and cargo pockets. One man carried his tiny baby in a cradle pack.

"The first buyer of a kilt was a 300-pound Seattle bouncer," a member of our group said. "Kilts appeal to men not afraid of their sexuality," explained another.

"It's not a fashion statement," insisted Sadie, a young woman in the swing, embroidering her sampler. "At Holden, you can wear whatever you want."

Can we also be whomever we happen to be–Japanese, Mexican, Jewish? My throat was clogged with anxiety. What good would it do to argue? If these villagers won't accept people as they are, they won't change their minds because of what I say. Yet Holden's Mission Statement makes it clear: "Celebrating the unity and diversity of the church, all humanity and all creation....This place apart is where all might find healing, renewal and refreshment." Most villagers have attended sessions on ethnic diversity and anti-racism, but not everyone gets it.

A young man came up the porch steps from the dining room with his plate filled with food, and sat where Ted had been. The interruption gave me a chance to leave, to walk down the hallway to our room and go over Cynthia's questions: "What enables us to do something alternative? What disables us so we can not?"

Easy to answer if it's about a man wearing a skirt, but not about ethnic cleansing. Could my old life-guard whistle blast these porch people out of their prejudices, with its shrillness? Could I announce the penalty: "You're on Dish Team duty until you change your attitude."

Cynthia's second question hung in the hallway just ahead of me: what disables you from doing such a thing? Fear. Of what? That they might ignore me, laugh off my threat, or not speak to either Ted or me for the remaining 20 days that we will be part of village life. And why does that matter? Because we can't handle any more troubles, since we have already been beaten senseless. I had never thought of our neighbor problems quite that way before.

Yet a new thought burst out: was this porch conversation a test of tolerance for the intolerant? Wasn't I intolerant of the neighbors? Look at my co-workers! I really didn't know them. I burst into our room and asked Ted, "Why did you leave?"

He looked up from his book. "I wasn't going to listen to that crap."

"Shouldn't we object to that crap?"

"What's the use? We're not going to change those people."

"That's 'what ought to be'."

"What do you mean?"

"Just something from Cynthia's class." I sat down on the bed beside Ted, where fresh air came in our window. "How would you categorize these people?"

"Bigots."

With nothing more to say or do, I knew we couldn't change neighbors at home, or here. Besides, did we want everyone to think like we do? That's egotistical, threatening, intolerant and impossible. Ted and I cannot change, avoid, or punish our neighbors. Those are hard facts. Here's another. We had flunked the true test: tolerance of the intolerant.

Journalist I. F. Stone, often called a radical, reminds us that "somebody has to fight these battles and lose and lose and lose until someday somebody who believes as you do, wins!" In one of the special newspapers for Holden's 40th anniversary, Tom Witt wrote how he came to live at Holden when he was five years old. Growing up in this environment, he remembered: "free exchange of ideas in a safe place. Adults asked pointed questions and disagreed – out loud – about important things. But it was okay!"

What would Witt have thought about our porch conversation? If our children and grandchildren had been there on the porch, would the conversation have been different? What would any of them think of Cynthia's class? At her next session I asked her: how can we love neighbors who are hateful of us, and others?

"That's a universal neighbor problem." Cynthia looked at me with a crooked smile. "It's a hard question. You have to discover what kind of action will show your love for them. You need empowerment to do that."

Her answer reminded me how difficult life in community is; how miserable we can make our own lives. Climbing a glacier seems easier, in comparison. Applying love-in-action to the porch situation, I might have to blow the whistle, even while I stood with trembling knees. Could I explain to the porch people that I couldn't stay but would like to exchange opinions another time? Without sounding stuffy and arrogant? Could I treat each guest honorably?

That empowering door needed to open for me to answer the ultimate question: will this love-in-action help me the next time my neighbor comes at me with his gun?

Aggressive Sociopaths:

(From The American Psychiatric Association)

...derive strong gratification from harming others. They like to hurt, frighten, tyrannize, bully, and manipulate for a sense of power and control....

Chapter Twelve
Sampling the Arts

If modern artists throw dung at the Virgin Mary, it shows they care.
William Dyrness, theologian

The morning-bus departure for the boat dock brought out a kitchen farewell-contingent of workers, decorated with garbage-like plastic on their arms. This absurd farewell honored Sara, the birthday girl who had become a popular member of the kitchen crew. Happy for her, I asked her to say hello to her Mom, and waved the busload away.

Ted and I, halfway through our Holden stay, saw our own farewell creeping up on us. Time slipped away in our spirited escape. I expected miraculous therapy from these wilderness weeks and it might be in the brewing stage. Some new concept of the universe, a spiritual break-through or this sampling of the arts will help us shrug off the years of neighborly abuse.

Yes, I'm talking miracles but not the message-from-heaven-kind. Still if I heard a mysterious voice calling my name, I would jump out of my sensible work boots. A correct answer, a solution, to our vendetta, could jettison us away from stormy clouds. Surely, we will find the right trail here.

Coming to terms with myself on this retreat, I concede that I am a housewife and have been for fifty years. With marriage came responsibilities: in charge of spider webs on the ceiling and stains in the toilet bowl. As a newlywed, and further down the line, none of that changes. Scrape off the veneer of a Ph.D. or title of Editor or founder of discussion groups, or one-hundred-mile cyclist, and at the center of my being I am a housewife.

On my kitchen wall are two icons that have followed me from the kitchen of our first house in Missouri to our present home on the Central Coast of California. Prints of Chardin's *The Kitchen Maid* and *The Blessing*, these pictures spoke to me during my first seventeen years as a housewife, and continue to appeal as time (and we) move on. I like the calmness and loving relationship between this kitchen maid, her domestic work, and her daughters. I cherish the rightness of this art with our present Japanese-style farmhouse, simple and basic. So, call me homemaker, domestic engineer, chaos coordinator and art appreciater.

Since childhood I dabbled in pastels and water colors, created a sand-paper mosaic, and transformed found-objects into a six-foot-board mountainous-skyline inscribed: *From whence comes my strength?* My architect-builder father could draw well. Judy, our oldest daughter became an artistic genius in cardboard carving, a new medium selling at $2000 a picture and winning awards. All of that is in my family gene pool, icing on my housewife cake, my base for any delights to come, including our breakthrough solution.

Ted and I took the last two seats at a round lunch table for eight and heard the name *Rossing*. Tom Rossing had been Ted's classmate at Luther College; both attended the same physics classes, bull sessions and beer-drinking escapades on weekends. I looked at the strong-jawed man sitting across the table from us. "Ted, could that be your friend, Tom?"

"Yes."

The two men were on their feet, shaking hands, 52 years after Tom and Ted had graduated and launched new lives. Effortlessly, Holden does this bringing together of people from our past.

Tom's booming and melodic voice cut through the luncheon buzz. He is a singer and musician, too. "Retired? No," he said. "Still teaching physics of music and acoustics at Northern Illinois University in DeKalb."

Ted answered with a laugh. "I've been retired for twenty years and never went back. Not even for a day."

Tom, wildly enthusiastic about his work, had taken the other path. "I use laser beams," he explained, "to show my students how musical instruments make sounds."

He pulled a photo out of his wallet. Oval circles covered a holographic image of a hand-bell. "That's what vibrations look like."

"It looks like a paisley design," I said.

Tom told us he would be an exchange professor in Scotland the coming fall. His wife Dolores said, "Come visit us there."

The Rossing family is formidable with two daughters ordained Lutheran ministers, and all members musically talented. Tom's son-in-law, here at Holden, planned to teach Singing for Non-Singers. When Volunteer-coordinator Roseann enthusiastically announced the name of the class, people in the dining room laughed.

"That's not so funny," groaned the smiling Roseann. "I know I'm going to sign up for it."

Dolores and I agreed to go, too. A gray-haired runner and cyclist, she shared interests with me, like Shi-Bashi and non-singing. We sat only inches from the concert grand piano where Tom's daughter, Karen, a pastor and pianist, sat poised to accompany this class of twelve Non-singers.

One introduced herself as a professional. "I'm here to pick up some teaching techniques."

Tom's son-in-law, a junior high teacher, exuded enthusiasm and ideas for us to try:

"Expand your belly.

"When singing, divide up diphthongs like: awa - y, fra-end, ye-ar.

"Singing is classy screaming. It's yelling. It's like giving birth to a calf."

We laughed, probably like his middle-school students. The only information I had remembered about singing came from a baritone, who taught English part-time with me a few years back. He claimed, "When I'm singing, and my breathing and everything is right, it's as good as an orgasm."

So we giggled, breathed, yelled and stood up to belt out the classic, *What a Fra - end We Have in Jesus*, with a jazzy beat. We non-singers sang. We opened our throats full throttle and sounded glorious. But sometimes my squeaks sounded like off-key yelling. At home I could practice in the shower or when driving alone, singing my way past the neighbors. I knew the human voice was a remarkable instrument; opera singers can project arias above a full orchestra.

At home, Ted joined me often to hear choral music, attend art exhibits and check out interesting buildings. Along with Ted's career in the Space Program as aeronautical engineer, he designed, helped build and maintain four of our homes, that we lived in for an average of 12 years each. So in retirement, he leaned toward construction, woodworking and design. Ted admired fabrics in good clothing and was curious about the firing of clay pottery. Therefore, we attended Holden's kiln opening, a new experience for us.

Villagers of all ages circled at the door of the imposing oven, encased in its own little house. Shirley and Gary, village potters in heat-resistant gloves and safety goggles, opened the propane-fired kiln. Steam drifted out. The two lifted out each bowl, cup, plate, figure and plaque to set them on a nearby bench.

As the artwork cooled, misty steam floated away and the diversity of shapes and muted colors held our attention. A large coffee mug beckoned for finger and thumb curling around its big handle. With its shiny black glaze, a big bowl glistened in the sun. An abstract, roundy figure begged for human hands to hold it, for comfort's sake.

Gary told the group, "We will pass the fired work around, from one person to another so you can feel the warmth that fired each piece, and the shape and curves the potter gave the clay. Very carefully, pass it to the next person as you become part of this process of making art."

The hands of the children looked too small for this responsible job. I worried that my gardening hands may not be clean enough to hold someone's precious work of art. Ted's hands shake because of his Essential Tremor. That doesn't limit his use of power tools in carpentry work but holding a cup steady can be difficult.

To place our sensitive finger tips and the fatness of our palms on newly fired pottery, we attendees stood in anticipation and reverence. The handling of each hot, newly-fired piece of clay spread around the circle, into the second row and onto the line of people that nearly turned the corner of the Village Center. No one backed away from touching the treasures. We pottery admirers murmured surprise at the warmth and simple beauty of each piece. This potters' art charged us like a spiritual-awakening revival.

But not everything had survived. Some pots broke in the overnight firing at 2000 degrees. One red-headed pre-teen wiped away her tears while picking up the pieces of her bowl. Maybe broken lives, changing relationships, surprising letdowns show up in our clay pots.

"No one knows why it happens," said Shirley, dark-haired and intense about art.

"Colors change, too," added Gary. "Sometimes there are big disap-pointments. This misplaced dab of indigo on the rim of my bowl ruins it."

He saw me admiring the dark blue serving dish. "You can have it for eight dollars."

I bought the flawed piece from Gary. The dab made it unique. The distinctive grace of this dark serving dish would show off a fresh-fruit salad. This opening of the kiln, buying of the bowl, and Tom's research into the physics of music, all merged to fight off any realities of the ugly, the belligerent.

More vibrations of artistry lured me on when Shirley announced a beginner class. "For three dollars, everyone gets a slab of clay to work with. I will show you how to make a bowl."

Eager kids, parents, guests and volunteers like me bought our squares. We flattened the brown material with a rolling pin, to begin "hand building." Shirley explained how using the wheel is more advanced. "John will demonstrate."

With every space crammed with pots and supplies, the shed's one empty corner made room for the potter's wheel and the talented apprentice. A lump of clay whirled around in the wheel head, emerging as a graceful vessel, one that I wanted to caress and place on a shelf to admire. My classmates breathed in this same fervor, eagerness for our first-time efforts.

A rolled glob of clay quickly became my leaf-like dish. I draped it over a form patterned from plates Shirley had made. She gave us tips for decoration: A tiny pine-tree sprig from the tree just outside the door pressed it's design into my clay dish.

Glazing and firing went fast. The next morning unveiling, even without a formal opening, excited me. My finished dish, with sky-blue and white bumpy surfaces, had survived. It emitted an earthy scent as I checked it out like a newborn. Wrapped in swaddling paper, the dish traveled in my hand to the little table by our window .

That evening Ted and I answered the village bell calling us for vespers. Structured religion had been the core of our family for forty years. I had learned much about social responsibility to the world from our pastors and church leaders, and gained a broad outlook on all religions. I was now a graduate who doesn't want to return to the classroom. My attendance at Holden's evening service usually lost out to a preference to be alone.

Love of humanity and environment equaled pure religion to me. That means responsibility to take care of the needs of the world. I take that seriously and hang onto many of Christ's ideas like turning the other cheek but lose interest in doctrine, creeds, traditions and rules. In many ways, I have been a good student in the school of Lutheran ideas, retaining important points. My "graduation" leads me into a wider world to try and act out those beliefs.

Time-honored institutions fail to speak to me now. Words about repentance, salvation, and heresy are scary concepts. I never cared for the word worship either because it sounded like groveling. What kind of God needs prayers from mortals? I prefer to float away as an un-tethered free spirit.

On Friday nights at Holden, I stayed away from the healing, candle-lighting vespers where about fifty villagers come forward to kneel at the central altar. I hoped the service worked for them, but I couldn't understand a God requiring such actions. If the petitioners for health believe the service heals them, such conviction might change body chemistry to make them well. That could be how it works. Ted often went on Fridays: "There's comfort in the service."

"Do you go up to the altar?"

"No, I stay in the audience."

"I would feel like at imposter at something like that."

"Then don't go."

"That's what I do."

Such conversations may sound like arguments but I don't dash out, slamming the door. Perhaps, Ted seeks strength to overcome the Vendetta, arrest, continued harassment. Each of our exchanges of ideas, I believe, bring new understanding, a form of showing interest. It's like the artist who threw dung – only not as dramatic or controversial.

When I attend vespers, my mind often wanders, even though the liturgy is imaginative, with great singers walking down the aisles belting out the hymns. Yet my roving mind leads me to study the large artistic banners hanging from a ceiling that has its own enormous mural. This art is not a bad thing for me to worship.

The huge bright-colored mural features outsized fantasy figures, biblical scenes and psychedelic designs. The painting covers the entire ceiling of this former gym, reaches down onto the walls of a narrow balcony for a Sistine Chapel effect. And that's the part that intrigues me.

Artistic villagers had designed and painted the mural, section by section, with left-over colors, many years ago. The finished mural resembles the art of Bosch, Dali and Picasso. One large design looks like paisley vibrations on a hand bell. Another scene resembles Dante's inferno. Modern cityscapes show us an overturned grocery cart, police helicopters, trash bins, plastic bags interwoven in chain-link fences, and neon signs. Abandoned cars rest in weedy lots.

But one part of the mural, where it dips into the balcony, perplexed me. I had stared many times at this edge: a flowing purple form confronting something abstract in green and yellow. Part of the mural appeared to be breaking through the ceiling, sliding down the side walls. Perspective demanded I put my hand on that spot, to know the wall and ceiling were really there. I extended the concept of the mural: Do we meet and merge with other lives, like walls and ceilings do? Does this artwork point to wounds in other lives, hurts that caused Ted's arrest?

Observant people often find identical designs in tree trunks and creek beds, clouds and rocks. Such replication seems eerie, like this mural that leaps away from the wall and disappears in the balcony.

After the non-singing class, with a few minutes before vespers, I grabbed the fragment of time to see if I had been misled by the artwork. Under the colorful banners, I walked up an old staircase leading to the narrow balcony, stepped around chairs stored there to find my purple blob. I could smell turpentine. The mural looked different here. These merging three colors lured my hand to follow the intersection of their structure. Fascination melded me into this part of the mural.

With my fingers, I found the curving seam with the ceiling, and knew I had been fooled. The artists had raised these images to a higher dimension than the rest, a secret that even they might not realize. The abstract design could be anything, or everything. This optical illusion of the mural became mine. No longer an outsider, I gratefully joined the art community. And faced my fear of going home to the place where purple meets the green and yellow.

When I came down from the balcony, Ted, in his dress-up slacks, was waiting at the door. Vespers would start in a few minutes. I told him about my artwork inspection. He said he had just finished his own woodworking art. "My rocking-chair project. The back kept coming apart from the armrest."

"Has the chair been broken for a long time?"

"A year! I just made a better joint, put in some gussets. It's back in the kindergarten."

"Gussets? That's a sewing term." I laughed, recalling how Ted had learned to use his mother's sewing machine when he needed sails for his iceboat. With his many home skills, he often exceeded the abilities of this so-called lifetime housewife.

Villagers streamed in both doors. Kids chased each other down the aisles. Dinner announcements had told us that for this week Holden had the largest group of kids under the age of six, that they had ever had. Their screaming was not classy. I preferred sitting by the creek, watching a deer amble down our road, a bear checking out a Holden trashcan.

" I'm leaving," I whispered to Ted and slipped out the door..

He caught up with me. "The noise is pretty bad."

"We've been through that with our kids," I recalled. "Remember when we sat in the second row at Village Church and Nancy put her bonnet on your head during the sermon?"

Laughing, we walked up the hill to check the bulletin board. Jazzed by my artistic encounter with the mural, I looked for some more exciting things on the calendar. One presentation that fit into our free time was taught by Ingrid, a woman I had talked to in the ice cream line that afternoon.

She had given a class based on Tillie Olsen's powerful piece, *As I Stand Here Ironing*. In the essay, the woman ironing bemoans her failed mothering of her only daughter. In spite of these strong emotions, she continues and finishes the ironing.

Ted pointed to Ingrid's next topic: "What Is Sex Good for?"

Baked Eggs Florentine

(Having guests? Try this recipe the next time
449 of your closest friends drop by for breakfast.)

72 pounds frozen spinach
4 ½ gallons of onions, diced
1 ½ gallons Parmesan cheese, grated
630 eggs
18 C cream or whole milk

Sauté onions until soft. Add spinach and season with garlic and black pepper. Sauté until mixture is heated throughout. Spread mixture in greased pans. Whip eggs, Parmesan cheese and cream (or milk) until well blended. Bake uncovered at 350 degree for 45 minutes to an hour.

Chapter Thirteen
What Is Sex Good For?

*The omnipresent process of sex...is the pattern of all the process
of our life.*
     The New Spirit, Havelock Ellis

A middle-aged man, standing with his friends by the bulletin board
the next morning, exploded about the "What Is Sex Good For?" topic.
This village guest, in his Bermuda shorts and sandals, sighed and objected,
"They'll say that sex isn't good for anything," he objected. "I could give
them reasons why sex is good."

Passing villagers stopped to look at the notice and at this irate man
who raised his voice to address all of us: "I could tell them what sex is
good for. Don't they know?"

His stunned audience watched him stride away and some of his friends
chuckled. But they all took note of time and place for this class. At three
o'clock, the Fireside Room was filled. Ted spotted his former classmate,
Tom and his wife Dolores on the other side of the room, in the front.
We found two chairs near the back.

Ted chuckled, "I don't want to be called on."

"You don't know what sex is good for?" I asked.

"Sure, fun and procreation."

But this group expected more details than that. With various ages,
cultures, and skin color in the room, it could be a lively program. Fellow
gardener, Sadie, sat crunched up with a book in the same corner with us.
In two days she was leaving Holden for the seminary, to study spiritual
counseling. I greeted her: "Hi, what are you reading?"

"It's a fortune-cookie game," she said. "It's about sex." Sadie's tone
implied that I was too old to understand such things. She never made
eye contact with me, but threw out one more remark: "The game's called
Between the Sheets, and uses a hymnal..."

Sadie spoke in a monotone. She made me feel like an imbecile who
didn't belong at this presentation and could not comprehend the innu-
endoes, double entendres, or spicy puns of her game.

Excitement buzzed around the room. Conversations climbed to higher
pitches. The panel assembled in front. One woman represented a Chicago rehabilitation program for prostitutes. For nine years, the project
had offered hope and rehab to more than 20,000 women. Twelve black
women from that program lived at Holden for the week as part of our

community. They usually hung around together but today they were scattered in the audience. Two were in our row.

Ingrid, a strong woman with an air of confidence, moderated the session. She started by reading a poem projected on the screen, with its words of tenderness, nurturing, caring. A tall woman with long gray hair, Ingrid turned to address our roomful of expectant, eager, sexual beings: "When we talk about sexual relations here, we include same-sex relations."

Well, OK. That fit with Holden's policy of complete acceptance of gays. In fact, during our first week, a bishop from Michigan had concluded well-attended seminars on homosexuals and the church.

Ingrid continued, "Usually, the term *oral sex* means something done to a penis. Not a clitoris, or other parts of female genitalia."

Our audience of a hundred or more scuffled their feet, examined their nails. This was strong talk from our moderator but no one left the room. They didn't want to miss anything. Ingrid introduced the panelists: a parent of teenagers, a therapist and the prostitute-rehab director, who looked least intimidated by our topic.

Each took a turn speaking but none of them addressed the subject: What Is Sex Good For? Instead, we heard of teen-age sexuality problems, and rehab for prostitutes who had suffered unspeakable lives.

The two from the Chicago project, in our row, listened intently to their project leader's presentation, as though they might be tested on the material. Possibly, they gave rapt attention to honor this woman who had rescued them. A dynamic speaker with lots of energy, the rehab leader tackled ideas such as God's original purpose for women as equal partners in the family.

Black women especially, she said, endure daily ravages of sexism as well as racism.

She spoke of prideful vocations, educational opportunities, goals and honors. The former prostitutes sitting near us looked calm and at ease. Being here in the village could be an important part of their recovery.

A Fuller Seminary professor, William Dyrness, wrote about Roualt's carnival-art of clowns and prostitutes. The professor says we must "see prostitutes in the tragic light of God's purpose for Eve." What interpretation of that purpose, I wonder, do we follow: companionship, partnership, breeding stock, or recreational sex?

Here at Holden Retreat Center, like anywhere on earth, people wanted to hear what sex was good for, but none of the panelists tackled the question. The summer's theme for Holden, *Forty Years in the Wilder-*

ness, might refer to our acceptance-level about sex. Audience energy dropped from high hopes to limp inattention. I suspected the majority of listeners had tuned out. Where was that man who had spoken out at the bulletin board? Difficult to spot him in this crowd and encourage him to speak. Sadie could tell us what she learned from her game. We desperately needed someone to get us back on the subject. Where was Alfred Kinsey when we needed him?

With his 1948 study on sexual behavior of the human male, Kinsey changed Americans' views about sex. A Harvard-educated zoologist, he used the scientific approach to help people break away from shame and fear of talking about sex. With an easy-going interviewing style, his teams unearthed hidden sexual practices that few people had talked about before.

When his study on women's sexuality came out in the 50s, the research showed varied sexual partners and swinging couples. Kinsey suffered from attacks on him for "destroying American values." Cultural debates sparked by this Kinsey Report, continue today.

Mulling over our question for the gathering, what is sex good for, various answers and questions spun around in my head. Sex is a mystery, not always the same, a great ending to one's day, or a beginning. Sex appeal attracts like a magnet and won't go away, even with age. It's healthy, good for your heart. Sex keeps us in touch with body, mind, soul, and our heritage of the human race, plus all creatures, geological and geographic wonders of the world. Sex is complete togetherness.

In the beginning of life, one amoeba broke into two parts. Didn't that start the urge for sexual re-union? The two amoebae parts came together sexually for "fun and procreation." Did the amoebas feel completeness?

An English monk, quoted in Tony Hendra's book *Father Joe* says: "Sex is a wonderful gift, a physical way to express the most powerful force in all existence – love. Sex is a brilliant idea of God's, I think, almost like a sacrament."

Father Joe says the first exercise of love is listening to another human for a beginning of understanding: "Listening is reaching out into that unknown other self."

To really hear what we say is what most women want. Good listening, as well as good dancing, leads to good sex as lovers scale guarded walls of individuality.

James Thurber's book, *Is Sex Necessary?* spoofs psychoanalysis. He praises the combination of sex and psychology for "staving off boredom."

An American judge ruled that James Joyce's *Ulysses* should be allowed in the U.S. "even though the theme of sex is in the minds of his characters continuously."

The judge added, "That's sickening, rather than an aphrodisiac. So the book will not be banned."

People have different ideas. In India, there are many self-chosen eunuchs, male and female, who no longer want a sex life, or children. They argue that they can devote more time to public issues than non-eunuchs, and have formed a powerful political party. In the accompanying photos in the newspaper, the embracing eunuchs show great affection for each other.

Why don't we talk about these varieties? Or take the time to consider cultures where wives provide procreation, but mistresses supply fun. As one mid-eastern man put it, "the lips that kiss my children good night, must be pure."

As for Ingrid's panel, the members forgot the original question. She turned to her listeners for queries. Tom had his hand up, waving. Ingrid called on him.

The physics-of-music professor brought us back to the subject: "Why doesn't anyone mention the benefits of masturbation?"

The audience became deadly quiet. Panicky facial expressions of the panelists indicated that their church panels at home didn't talk about such things. No speaker tackled Tom's query. They looked at the ceiling, hung back in their chairs, passed the question onto Ingrid. The audience hushed, appeared attentive once again.

"We can't cover everything in one hour. Next time we'll have classes for a week. And I'm all for masturbation. But now our time's up." Ingrid thanked the panel and it was over.

As we moved out of the room, to accommodate the next presentation, a young man came up to Tom and said, "That was an important question you asked. A good one."

But the spell was broken. Neither he nor Tom pursued the topic. In fact, the really hard question that even Kinsey admitted scientific research can not answer, is where sex ends and love begins.

Some say love spills over in the process of Creation, and exists everywhere, in everyone and everything. So we can see love as at-one-ness with creation. This omnipresent love is experienced in sex, recognized in the spirit of our beloved. Sex is loving attention. Sex is like laughter. De Chardin suggests, "Give it all; do not hoard goodness."

In a recent AARP (American Association of Retired Persons) article, the magazine interviewed some prominent couples who had been married fifty or more years. Carl Reiner explained that he always tried to make his wife laugh.

His wife Estelle, a former scene designer, answered, "I don't think you *try* to make me laugh!"

"We still hold hands," Carl said. "So we don't fall."

Estelle laughed.

Former president Jimmy Carter answered AARP's question about "lust in his heart" (covered in a 1976 *Playboy* interview), "Yes, but only for Rosalyn"

Both of them smiled when she answered, "And only for Jimmy."

The Carters believe in love at first sight. Jimmy explains: "The morning after my first date with Rosalyn, my mother asked what I had done the night before. I answered, 'Went to a movie with the girl I'm going to marry.'"

Yet their marriage nearly broke up when they argued about a book they wrote together.

Rosalyn recalls hanging up the phone on her husband after she had said, "I've had a bad day and you can go to Hell."

Long-term-marriage research at University of California at Berkeley, uses the term Relationship Maintenance Behavior, to talk about marriage. They received answers like these:

"We act cheerful when together."

"I enjoy discussing our relationship with my husband."

"I could have married any number of other women but I stuck it out with her."

Did the researchers want answers about sexual relations? Reality seems remote in such scientific language: Relationship Maintenance. The Berkeley group also found that long-term couples who spent time with the spouse's relatives rated high on this "relationship-maintenance." But what did that academic phrase mean?

For the first nine summers of our marriage, Ted and I traveled from Missouri to Minnesota's Lake Minnewasca to stay with his mother for two weeks. Our family loved the lake view and quick access from her porch, and small-town charms of Glenwood. I didn't know it was relationship-maintenance at the time, but believe now it was.

With a family of three small children, I found it difficult to spend that much time with my mother-in-law, in spite of what research says about maintenance. Upset one night, I yearned to drive our old Jaguar around that lake and squeal the tires on every curve. Maybe I'd drive it off the boat ramp into the lake.

I didn't do any of those things. But according to the research, those nine summers of in-law visiting, increased my chances of a long, happy, well-maintained marriage.

Middle-term marriages (20 to 30 years) fail more than any other group, researchers show, and ours received help from Marriage Encounter. This movement took the San Fernando Valley by storm in the 1970s, when Ted and I had been married 20 years. To experience the Marriage Encounter weekend meant being away from home and children. The two-day experience showed us how to make our marriage stronger.

Participants were like-minded couples with healthy relationships. Marriage Encounter couples, mingling in the halls of the lovely convent where we stayed, did not greet each other. That was a rule that seemed strange at first. Couples listened to talks together, wrote love-letters to each other in privacy, and dialogued later in our rooms. That was the first time I had ever seen Ted cry.

Being an engineer and a Scandinavian, Ted fit the stereotype of seldom displaying emotion. But the intensity of topics and the focused format made a difference. Our first subject for writing a love letter was "How Would I Feel if You Died?" That was when we knew that Marriage Encounter was running deep with its love letters.

Two weeks before our wedding, we had written many love notes. Obsessed with fixing up the three-room flat we had rented, I scrubbed and scraped during the day while Ted worked at his new engineering job. My daily scribbling on a pad listed for him my tasks of the day. He returned from work to paint the walls in the evening, for he had moved in. I lived with my parents who said they didn't want us to be there together in the evening. I wrote: "Please forgive me, Ted, but over-protective parents are preserving the family name..."

From Ted: "You're a doll for working here. I'll blow the room full of kisses so that maybe a few will be lingering here when you arrive. Love, Ted."

In Marriage Encounter, we wrote entirely different letters. Our leaders suggested we use similes and metaphors, and we needed to show great interest in discussing the assigned topic together. We wrote for ten minutes. Ted and I had never discussed death, especially ours, during our ritualistic Friday night gatherings with a bottle of wine. To write the truth, about our despair and then admit to a surprising feeling of relief at the death of our spouse, shocked us. Both of us ended up in tears, with Ted leading the way.

After another intense preparation session on the Weekend, I wrote:

> ...*the support of the prayer couples and the music was beyond words. It's unreal that this is happening to me but the entire room must have been charged as I saw others with handkerchiefs to their eyes. To their question, How do you feel about going on living? there has never been any doubt as to living for me or for us. If there are uncertainties, doubts, boredom, etc., at times, there are still too many sunsets to see with you, too many Friday evenings, sailing trips, bicycle trails, camping sports...to be experienced.*
>
> Ted answered: *Yes, Barb, even the sex is in some way different each time, more intense, a new sharing and at that moment we are different persons than ever before or ever again. Any emptiness must be a deadness within me...your liveliness has opened my mind to the wonders... I couldn't let on too obviously but you are a strength...and I can see why this question can take so long to answer...there are many balloons to release. I like the phrase that love is a daily decision.*

That was also a rare time for Ted and me to come together sexually in the middle of the day. How exciting for us to think that most of the other couples did the same thing.

These Marriage Encounter letters, I believe, launched us on our way to a Golden Wedding anniversary, and Holden Village. The day after Ingrid's presentation marked our anniversary date, celebrating 50 years of co-habitation, sex, children, romantic evenings, arguments, love. My plan was to whisper *I love you* fifty times in Ted's ear during the day. The 5:30 alarm signaled the first ten whisperings. Ted didn't have to get out of bed till six.

Hardly anyone in the village knew the day was our 50th and we wanted it to be low key, ordinary. In fact, that day was my turn to clean the community bathroom on our floor in the lodge. I mopped and sanitized showers and floor, using some magic potion in a special bottle. All of this, even though I had proclaimed to Yeshua, "I don't mop."

In checking the duty list in the dining hall, I saw that Ted and I had missed our dish-team turn the day before. I whispered in Ted's ear during coffee break. *I love you. I love you. We forgot dish team.*

Ted grimaced. "That was Holden's anniversary present."

No one, that I could tell, noticed my whispering, or chastised us for missing dish team. Next came ten whispers at lunch and at ice cream time in the afternoon. I had said the magic words forty times by then.

Ted and I were late to dinner and couldn't find a table with two empty seats. Wouldn't people be surprised to learn that Golden Wedding celebrants didn't even eat dinner together? Would they be surprised that we knew what sex is good for?

I sat at a long table by the door with Japanese volunteers, students from Kyushu. They all bowed to greet me. I bobbed my head, too, and told them I had lived in Osaka for nearly a year.

Mai, pretty with long, shiny hair, was the only woman in the group. I told her that Ted and I had spent Christmas in Kyushu, ten years previously, enjoying the natural hot springs. She said she was homesick. We both bowed when we parted.

On the way to our room, Ted and I saw the group of young black women from Chicago getting ready to jump rope. We stopped to watch, intrigued by the rhythmic steps and chants. It seemed to be their after-dinner ritual, on the sidewalk outside the dining hall. I wondered how they would have answered the question, *What is sex good for?* Would they have said, "Are you kidding? I've been beaten and tortured for sex. I don't see anything good about it." Or would some say, "I miss the fucking."

The jumping-rope may have been a symbol of their lost childhood. They played double-Dutch and double-Irish, and Red Hot Peppers, delightful to watch. People walked around them and smiled. One man tried double-Dutch jumping with them but had trouble getting started.

Everything was in the timing, as I recalled.

Ted and I watched from a distance. Just when I worked up my nerve to ask if I could try, they quit. The women rolled up the rope and disappeared into the night.

Marv and Nancy knew it was our anniversary. "We'll bring over a bottle of Marv's red wine," said Nancy. "He made it and it's good."

"OK. We'll get some glasses from the dining hall.

Ted sat in the one chair we had in our room. Marv, a big guy, sprawled on Ted's bed and opened his wine, releasing a wonderful fruity scent. Nancy and I arranged pillows so we could sit on my bed and lean against the wall. Nancy told us that as part of her job at the investment firm, she would be in San Francisco next spring. "And I will come down and visit you."

"Great. Marv, too?"

"No," he said, "I'll be on a working trip to Africa to build homes."

Marv told us how some native workers were quite inventive when they were all trying to restore a gutted hospital in Liberia. Marv praised Mr. Peewee, a Liberian who "got up on the walls with a ball of string and soon had the entire roof laid out. It was amazing to look down the edge and see how straight the lines were."

Draining the wine bottle, we cleaned up the last crumbs of power bar, served in my leaf-shaped, hand-built pottery plate. Ted taped Marv & Nancy's mountain-view anniversary card on the outside of our door, as they left. We hadn't talked about what sex is good for, about ameban romance, or the term *relationship maintenance*. I still had ten more *I love yous* to deliver.

Muesli

8 C rolled oats, dry
15 C six-grain cereal
½ C sesame seeds
½ C coconut
2 C raisins
2 C dried fruit
2 C dates
3 C nuts

Combine ingredients. Makes approximately 2 gallons, plenty to store and share.

Chapter Fourteen
The Comic and the Sacred

...a good land...flowing with streams, with springs and underground waters...and from whole hills you may mine copper...
Deuteronomy 8:7-9

To begin our day-off hike to Honeymoon Heights, Ted and I walked under whipping flags. The banners from many nations, one on each building, reminded us we're still in the world though in this wilderness. From Sweden's yellow cross, Mexico's green/white/red flag to Japan's rising sun and others, the flags speak of our role as good neighbors.

We took the upward trail through the woods, past an 18-foot swath cut by yearly avalanches, to find the honeymooners' huts. At Holden's small museum, next to the abandoned foundry, a docent told us, "About a dozen mining engineers, lonely in their wilderness jobs, found brides in nearby towns, and sometimes as far away as Seattle and Portland."

The friendly woman said the engineers had lived in the dorms: "The prospective bridegrooms turned these old mining huts into homes. You can see them for yourselves."

After seventy years of harsh winters, averaging 125 inches of snow, these tiny dwellings no longer looked hospitable. Ted didn't have his tape measure with him, but nevertheless estimated that, "they don't look big enough for two people."

A dented hot-water heater lay on the ground. "Has this been out here all these years?"

"Maybe they gathered round it to drink their hot-buttered rum." Ted had heard that the booming mining village had been the largest single customer of the Washington State Liquor Commission. "Or they hung out in the pool hall or bowling alley."

Pictures at the museum had shown happy brides, all smiles, ready for their wild adventure of marriage. They survived the Great Depression by roughing it in the wilderness at the same time. Their daily trudge to the village from these heights crossed two avalanche paths.

Honeymoon Heights route led us across mountains of copper tailings, orangey-yellow mining garbage that covered a third of the southern wall of Railroad Creek Valley. Piled up in the first fifty years of the twentieth-century, this waste marked an active time of prospecting and mining here and ecology was ignored. Now negotiations (started in 1999) continue between the mine company and regulating agencies Seeping water from under the tailings affect Railroad Creek, give it an orange color, reduce number of aquatic insects, which cuts fish population. The clean-up process is expensive and complicated with a cut-off wall, water collection system, and much more.

How big was the mound of tailings when the honeymooners set up housekeeping? They might be surprised to see baby alder trees growing in some spots on the pile, and a frisbee-golf course on another part. Did they ever quote Deuteronomy to justify their mining copper here? Did they celebrate the good land, flowing streams and springs?

According to many Native Americans, the power to recognize what is sacred enables them to face their futures. Sacred sites, objects, and the bodies of their ancestors through the ages, underlie important traditions. Holden qualifies as a similar sacred site for me because of its natural beauty, healing powers and provocative challenges.

Newcomers at Holden often gasp when they hear the Bible quote that seems to describe Holden Village right down to the mining of copper. Historians, however, say the passage was written before the copper age, and the mining part is an error. Environmentalists like John McPhee have called copper mining an enormous mistake: "Mining here in this most beautiful piece of country we've got, is like strip mining the Garden of Eden."

Leaving the Honeymoon Huts with each turn of our upward hiking path, Ted and I gained cameo images of our distant village. Old ski-pole walking-sticks anchored our high-stepping pace to view the panorama that migrating birds might see. Mountain ridge-tops hidden from the valley, peeked through neighboring spires at this higher level. Landscapes worthy of a fine Japanese woodcut showed deep shadows etched in ridges between the sun pockets. On this honeymoon- heights trail, one could believe that these rocks, on this land, have souls.

For our honeymoon in August 1952, Ted had reserved a fifth-floor walk-up attic room in a frame Victorian resort hotel on Lake Michigan. We had driven up from Missouri in his old Nash. Our room seemed perfect with distant views of the lakeshore. We never thought of the hazard of this aged building till the whole thing burned down a few years later.

What I remember is moonlight spilling into our room as we sat naked at the open window. We ate fresh pears bought at a roadside stand and thought the world was ours. At breakfast time, we wondered if the people at other tables could tell we were honeymooners.

In North St. Louis, our three-room flat awaited us, at $33-a-month rent-control. Prospects looked good: married, owned a car, with Ted's new engineering job at $5000 a year. We didn't have to worry about avalanches or copper prices, or bears at the garbage bin.

After the Honeymoon Huts, Ted and I chose the highest spot to sit, look, and eat sandwiches brought along. Nestled below, the village showed its main road, in and out of groves to ball park and labyrinth. Would the honeymooners have been surprised by today's labyrinth?

Some couples could still be alive, though a hundred years old. Did they stay married to celebrate their fiftieth? Two days after our own anniversary, we ate in peace on the mountain. It was a golden time for feeling blessed, cared for, favored to be here, wondering what comes next.

It seemed likely that we could discover our place in the universe if we looked long enough at these ridges. We might find new paths, gifts or bombshells. I needed to take home the up- lifted, inspired images. Memories of this wildness could blot out my vengeful impatience. Laura Blumenfeld's book shows that revenge is subjective, personal and I could feel my proprietary, vengeful grip. She also observes that the Mafia in the U.S. never "accepted the government monopoly on revenge." I had never considered our lawsuit against the neighbor's vendetta and actions as revenge. Fairness was what we wanted.

It's not our fault that the Gnome suffers post-traumatic-stress-syndrome and the Witch assails us for "starting our family while he was fighting for our freedom in Vietnam." How could we ever answer that charge?

Advice that I've read for such veterans runs to their reading any self-help book that "jumps off the shelf," or finding a hobby, a focus. (We had become the gnome's "hobby".) Advisors say, "Don't close down, develop new learning paths, express yourself."

One of our acquaintances had been head psychiatrist at the Veteran's Hospital in Los Angeles. He offered to help us with our neighbor problem, but I really wanted to talk to the counselor the Gnome saw on a regular basis. Did the Gnome brag about the harassing tricks he played on us? Or did he claim we were doing those things to him? I didn't know the proper way to handle such a request, so did nothing. We told only a few of our friends about the arrest and felony charge.

God does not cause unfairness, many pundits claim, or disasters, harassment, war or the Holocaust. Let's stretch that idea with a question: "If not God, then who controls such things?" Answers could run from *No one is in control*, to *We are all in control*, and all the way to *God doesn't know what's going to happen, any more than we do.*

Starting down from the mountain lookout, Ted and I fought gravity to keep our balance on the steep pebbly path. Senses alerted, we danced through the trail dangers to cruise into the village as rain began to fall. Maybe the rain could control the fire hazard.

Spitting clouds brought celebration to our dry land. Children danced on the main street as we came by, their faces turned up toward the welcoming water. "Rain, rain, don't go away."

"Let's swim in the raindrops."

"Let's drink it." The celebrants opened their mouths.

Villagers came out to spin between the pitter-pat, to dance, to inhale and worship the earthy smell of water and dust. A young couple practiced their duet for vespers under the metal roof of the dining hall's porch. The weeping sky kept the beat.

"Our deep valley looks different close up," I said, "cozy, less wild in this gentle storm."

"It would be a nice time," Ted admitted, "to visit a honeymoon hut for a hot drink."

As part of the Founder's Day festivities, Norm in his purple robe, would read the astonishing letter written forty years ago by founder Wes Prieb, a Bible-institute student. He had written letters for three years to the defunct mining company, expressing great interest in its remote town for sale. Advertised at $100,000 as a possible ski resort, the 1000-acre property, leased from the Forest Service, contained 14 chalets, 6 barracks, hotel/dining-hall/kitchen, and gym with pool hall and bowling alley. Wes Prieb said the place would make a great youth camp.

Copper prices had dropped 22 cents a pound and the money-strapped mining company answered Prieb's third letter, which asked, "Why don't you give the village to the Lutheran church?"

The mining company said yes.

"Sometimes I feel it was a shame," said Holden's first director, Carroll Hinderlie, "that God gave a gift like this to God's least imaginative people, the Lutherans."

Hinderlie proved himself most imaginative when he headed the first summer program with its theme of Holy Hilarity. The comic and the sacred prevailed for the next forty years in this wilderness, defining the new community at Holden. One of Martin Luther's apocryphal quotes defines community in this novel way: "Community is when my wife and I make love, and I think of you and your wife making love."

That statement must have been a show stopper in the 15th century when newly-wed Luther (with former nun, Kate, as his wife) might have made the analogy. Six centuries later, when Holden's director used the example, did he explain his theories about "revelry being grounded on reverence and banter couched in love"?

From the start, church members came to the early gatherings with jokes and joy as well as serious concerns. They found plenty of work, as well as fun, and went home as changed people. One of our pastors at Holy Shepherd in the San Fernando Valley came to Holden as part of a teenager-work-party. Later Pastor Jim told our congregation, "That was when I decided to be a pastor."

In the Holden fashion, Jim's congregation often came up with hilarious, maybe bizarre activities. Memories recall Ted appearing with five other men from the church council, each dressed in bra and tutu, to dance the Fantasia ballet at a talent show. Ellie, a former-ballet-dancer rehearsed them unmercifully until they almost got it right, making the episode a winner. An astonished audience cheered the men, now proud of their dance.

Our pastor's continued enthusiasm for community spirit, fun, hard work, and spiritual stretching, had influenced Ted and me to spend time at Holden fifteen years ago. We liked being remote and out of the loop of daily life at home. That helps us villagers see the world more clearly.

Japan's *Newsweek* magazine recently described the village as "a social and ecological alternate to materialism." The article quoted director Diane: "A Buddhist would probably be more comfortable here than a fundamentalist Christian. Our mission is 'out there.'" The magazine defined Holden as "a place where doctors and artists alike come for weeks or months, cleaning toilets and composting garbage, teaching classes or fixing roofs for nothing more than room and board."

Villagers' enthusiasm for Holden's attic, atop the Village Center and crowded with racks of clothes, reminded me that the Founder's Day parade was the next day. Dozens of would-be paraders pawed through formal gowns, clown outfits, tuxedos, fake-fur coats, and flowing colorful robes. Could some of the clothes have come from the mining families?

These people left immediately when the mine closed, forgetting dishes on the table and perhaps, these clothes in their closets.

A pre-teen girl held up a slinky black dress. "Mom, can I wear this?"

"What does that have to do with the theme?" asked the mother who looked at a bear costume with a long zipper down the torso. "This would be better."

"What theme?" asked the daughter, checking the black dress for length.

"Forty Years in the Wilderness," the mother answered.

A bright red, yellow and blue jester top, with pointy hemline and sleeves became a possibility for me. Maybe not about the theme either, but I took it. What about a hat? I had seen a many-tasseled hat in a pile on a table. A boy now had that hat on his head.

"It looks great," said his mother, and they walked out the door with my hat.

I should have come here earlier. Another pile of hats on a shelf caught my eye. Wedging myself between two young boys, I dug into the red/clown wigs, berets, cowboy hats, and found a cone-shaped cap. There were no mirrors in the room to check it's effect so I looped its rubber-band chin strap around my wrist, and left the attic with my parade costume.

What a fun place. I could wear a different costume every day for my last week at Holden. Or put on something new for each meal, select an outfit appropriate to the next class I attended. I would never do that at home. In fact, when wearing spandex biking clothes, I kept a raincoat in my car to conceal my *different* outfit when I stopped to run errands.

Now I lusted after one of those comical red wigs and promised myself to wear one before I left. A hidden sense of comic and sacred broke through my crust. After all, the word *humor* is in Holden's articles of incorporation, and how many corporations can say that?

Dressed like a jester at 6:00 am, I watered flower boxes on the second-floor porch of Lodge Six. Looking unusual in this bright top with its handkerchief hemline that dipped to the knees of my jeans, I topped off my large pointy hat with a sun visor. It seemed right, even expected on Founder's Day.

"Like your get up." said an elderly man who tapped his cane up the steps of the lodge.

A child asked me, "Are you a clown?"

"Just for the parade," I said.

"You volunteers have more fun that we do," said a woman guest who often chatted with me while I worked. I should have told her that "holy worldliness" is the reward, a theologian claims, for those who talk to gardeners.

After watering the flowers at Lodge One, I slipped into our room to use the marking pen for my Holy Hilarity sign to carry in the parade. Ted was leaving for work. "What's that you're wearing?"

"My parade costume."

"Glad I don't have to be in the parade. Actually, I've been asked to be in a play."

"What play?"

"I don't know. Some biblical story. I'm Boaz."

"Boaz? Didn't he cavort with a young, beautiful, wealthy widow?"

"I don't know."

"How many lines do you have?"

"Not a one."

"Who's playing Ruth?" I finished lettering my sign on a piece of scrap wallboard.

"Don't know. Don't even have to practice. Norm said just show up 15 minutes early for vespers. They'll have my costume and tell me where to kneel."

"Doesn't Ruth sleep at your feet, under your blanket, or something like that?"

"You know more than I do." He laughed and left for work. "See you at the parade." Our parade route was a short three blocks. Spectators would be few because most villagers were parading, in costumes from the attic. With Forty-Years-in-the-Wilderness theme, the parade brought out tie-and-dye outfits and other ideas from the sixties. The sturdy Hike Hauss women from Alaska, in borrowed formal outfits looked like Junior Prom candidates. CJ, who worked in the laundry, wore a little hat with a veil, threw a fur over the shoulders of her suit with its straight skirt, and showed off her high heels and white gloves. Dave, our Head Waitri, with wig, flower behind his ear, and make-up became a glamorous woman. He had to tell everyone, "I'm Dave."

"Dave?"

"Really."

Margaret had a sign: 20 YEARS IN THE TOILET. She carried bathroom brushes. "It's about equal rights for women libbers and bra burners."

Jonathon from teaching staff, had been up all night making a one-man float, a painted cardboard in the shape of a deer. Over six feet tall, Jonathon could still bend over inside his float to walk it in the parade. The message, a pun written in white paint, said *First Foundeer* with the second E floating above the word *Founder*. Wes Prieb would agree that deer lived here before miners, Lutherans, volunteers and celebrants of Founder's Day.

A light wind fluttered the international flags along Main Street and the parade began to the beat of the drum circle. Guitarists, buglers, and flute players added melodies and jazz. Flower children handed out daisies, chanting:

"What do we want? Peace. When do we want it? Now."

Jonathan's Foundeer loped by, surrounded with hullabaloo, corny showmanship, and a Mardi Gras feeling of abandonment. This little parade mingled with spectators, detoured into the crowd where there was one. We danced, sang and clapped, waved and blew kisses, surprised people and made them giggle. As Hinderlie had advised, "We should all act like rescued prisoners and laugh."

This gift of celebration was sacred, absurd, over too quickly, full of spectacle. For example, following Founders' Day dinner, we celebrated with the ultimate 70-foot banana split.

Jerry and his ice cream crew built two 35-foot troughs of aluminum foil, propped up on tables, filled with an array of flavors: Vermont Blackberry, Death by Chocolate, White Chocolate Chip, Black Walnut, Brazilian Coffee, Cherry Vanilla, Egg Custard. Nearby tables held bananas, toppings, bowls and spoons for a do-it-yourself feast, a scrumptious mess. By the time the bell rang for vespers, nothing remained in the trough.

A happy crowd wandered down the hill to hear Norm, in his purple cape, narrate the Bible story/play. I went to see Ted play Boaz, whose name means strength. During the day I had learned that Boaz gave permission to Naomi and Ruth, both newly widowed, to glean his fields. Naomi reminded her daughter-in-law that Levitic law required that male relatives of the deceased must marry the widow, in order to produce a son close to the genetic make-up of the deceased husband.

Naomi wanted that grandson and nudged Ruth: "Boaz is a relative."

The Village Center packed in 400 or more people, including hyperactive children playing tag in the aisles. Spotlights shone on Boaz, Naomi and Ruth. They wore costumes that I recognized from the attic. Ted looked magnificent with his grey beard, bald head and a colorful, flowing robe. I couldn't get a good look at Ruth.

132

Norm read the story from the Book of Ruth: Boaz, who already had one wife, agreed to marry Ruth. I wondered about that remarrying rule, if it applied to us in our tribes. Ted would have married his sister-in-law fifteen years ago when his older brother died. For those who worry about marriage rules in heaven, would Ted still be his sister-in-law's husband as well as mine? And would she be married to both brothers?

The main themes of the Boaz story, Norm explained, included living by the law, inclusiveness, loyalty and work. With her gleaning, Ruth showed the importance of all kinds of work, a dignified, respected activity, much more than servant hood. Volunteer workers at Holden often discuss that theme of work, with words like passion, sharing, service, necessary, meditation, community building, a call, and responsibility. Then they add "confusion, guilt, being overwhelmed and consumed."

Tired by the festivities, Ted and I walked slowly up the hill to Lodge One after vespers. Something seemed different. The village looked drab after all the colorful hoopla of the day. Our lodge looked plain. Ted pointed to the empty flagpole holder. "The flag's missing."

I checked the two lodges next to ours. "Their flags are gone, too."

Ted sighed.

When the money had been stolen, in this place where doors are never locked, that represented the first theft in forty years of on-your-honor and no-keys policy. This transgression with the flags raised my voice into a wail: "Is this a joke or bad dream? Is nothing sacred?"

Snickerdoodles

(AUTOGRAPHED Aug. 2002: *These are fun and yummy, even when you make 1500 of them!* Adriann)

1 1/4 C margarine
2 ½ C sugar
2 eggs
1/3 C milk
1 1/4 tsp vanilla
3/4 tsp cream of tartar
2/3 tsp bing soda
4 ½ C flour

Cream margarine and sugar. Add eggs, milk, vanilla, cream of tartar, baking soda and beat well. Add flour and mix. Form teaspoon-sized balls and roll them in a cinnamon and sugar mixture. Put on an un-greased cookie sheet and flatten with a glass. Bake at 350 degrees for 8 minutes; be careful not to over bake them. They should be soft when you take them out of the oven. Let the cookies cool for 2 minutes before removing from pan. Makes about 4 dozen cookies.

Chapter Fifteen
The Dream Catchers

They thought of their old, best dreams. F. Scott Fitzgerald

A feathery, willow-hooped sacred dream-catcher had decorated the rear-view mirror on a second-hand jeep that Ted and I bought a few years ago. I had hoped the beaded decoration came with the car. But the Native American student-owner took down her treasure: "I need this. My bad dreams get caught in the middle, but sacred dreams flow around the web, to me."

The front windshield looked bare without her keepsake. Ted's arrest and time in jail was a bad dream that should have been "caught in the middle." I envied cultures where families talked about their dreams at breakfast.

Ted and I finished our granola in Holden's dining hall while I told him my dream from the night before. "It was comic-book style with primary colors. The cartoon characters' dialogue appeared in white balloons."

He sipped steaming coffee while my dream-story leaped with flames toward a lineup of girls that included me. "Frightening!" I told Ted, "all of us drew back from a big incinerator. A white balloon escaped from my mouth screaming, 'Yikes!'"

Ted checked his watch, eager for the carpentry shop. "This really happened?"

"No. Well, yes! It's a rerun-dream from childhood, dreaming it twice and I knew it was a rerun. And now, last night!"

He wasn't really listening but I went on. "You've seen the old photo of my gym class at Turner Hall where we lined up according to height? I was seven or eight. In this childhood nightmare, my gym teacher chases me through rooms filled with ladders, balance bars, ropes and leather-covered gymnastic forms. The leader's white balloon shouts, 'You must learn the crab position on the rope.'"

The two of us carried our breakfast dishes to the kitchen counter. This lucid dream became a message waiting since childhood. Did my dream warn against a brush fire at Holden, or disaster at our home? My mind kept asking questions. I really didn't know the ropes.

On camping trips, I entertain dreamy memories while lying in my sleeping bag. With body relaxed in new ways, gravity pulls my bones, muscles, everything visceral down beyond my thinly inflated pad and pup-tent floor. This essence of me sinks through that floor to skitter across our rain-tarp into the earth. Mind, brain and soul plunge downwards.

Sometimes the names of fellow students emerge, and where they sat in Miss Seidel's eighth-grade class. Other times I review trips (California when I was eight), summer jobs (office work in a laundry at 19), and adventures (ten months teaching English in Japan when I was 62).

Memories about our marriage pop-up beginning with my first meeting with Ted Johnson from Minnesota, in Washington University's parking lot in St. Louis. We sailing-club members had gathered for a day on the Mississippi River. Later Ted told me he judged my long arms as "looking OK, which meant you probably had nice legs."

His legs didn't interest me as much as his being from "somewhere else" because I wanted to leave Missouri. Ted studied graduate-level nuclear-physics at the university; my foot had just entered the door at Gardner Advertising Agency downtown.

Ted's family considered me a Southern Belle, complete with a "Mammy." Not true! But my background was different from the small-town, farm heritage of Ted's family. And there was my olive skin, darkly tanned in summer. With brown eyes and hair, I was not Nordic but the "dark one," not to be fully trusted, maybe even feared.

To make matters more difficult, my mother sometimes disparaged rude people by referring to them as "farmers." Yet Ted's farm work meant he knew how to fix everything, make furniture, work on cars and build houses.

Before we left Holden's dining hall, co-director Dianne finished her announcements with unsettling news: someone had taken the international flags from all the Holden buildings. "We don't know why," she said. "Was it a prank or a political statement?"

The dining room quieted. Children stopped crunching their toast. Intensity showed we took this theft personally. Who were the flag-snatchers, and how did they do it? Did these moon rakers sneak up the squeaky wooden stairs during vespers to yank flags out of their holders? Did they re-march our Founder's Day parade at midnight with stolen flags waving in some kind of time-warped bubble?

Dianne continued: "Volunteers in Seattle made our beautiful flags. Knowing these women as I do, they will sew another set but please, don't make them work so hard."

My gaze swept over villagers at nearby tables. If someone had looked guilty, what would I have done? Dianne ended her message: "We ask that the flags be returned as soon as possible. And we offer anonymity, no punishment."

My mind traveled in a different direction from Dianne's. Something in me wanted justice, revenge, punishment on the village square. I would line them up with the gnome and witch and hurl the first stone. How could these tricksters sully the trust they had been given and steal our "one world" emblems?

Yet Dianne's offer enthralled me: if-you-did-it, make-amends, we'll-forget-it. Holden stood behind its pledge that even flag-thieves could be whomever they happened to be. Such generosity took me home.

Daydreaming with imagination, I hear the Gnome and Witch apologize with words in cartoon-like balloons: "We will make amends for our harassment and our lies to the deputies."

I heard flags whip in the wind at this glorious moment when it was my turn to answer: *We'll forget what you have done to us.* But the white balloon pointing to my mouth remained empty. Flags drooped and I could not talk forgiveness, even in my pipe dream.

Instead, my mind-screen showed me each harassment inflicted by the neighbors, over and over. After the segment of the Gnome throwing rocks at my jeep, appeared a small, corner-of-the-screen insert: I am explaining to the deputy, a big guy, how I heard the rock hit my passenger door and looked in the rear-view mirror to find the Gnome darting behind a tree.

Back to full screen, the deputy finds the dent in the door and warns the Gnome: "If you do that again, you will have to deal with me."

For the rest of this fantasy, I describe obstacles, broken gates, trucks parked in the way, a forest of Keep Out signs. But no one listens.

Ted had gone off to work, and my lawn sprinkler needed attention. Adjusting its spigot, I skipped from neighbor troubles to adventure-comic style sixty years-ago. My brother George and I had studied lurid covers of comic books in a drugstore, on Sundays while waiting for a streetcar to church. Any connection between our Unitarian Sunday School hour, and those ten minutes examining comic covers was never clear to me.

Flames, knives and ray-guns threatened comic-book cover-girls who fell off cliffs or faced steam-rollers. The cover-art scared and worried me about what to do in such dilemmas. George and I never discussed these spandex-dressed women, villains and heroes, or their problems. We didn't talk about Sunday School either. But my big brother was nicer to me after we'd been to church, because of one influence or the other.

Here at Holden, I weeded the iris bed, deadheaded dry blooms, exchanged stares with a deer who walked by, and I moved the sprinkler. I thought about the drugstore comic-book art style in my recent dreams. Why did it come back now?

Sleeping next to the same person for fifty years must influence dreams. Ted's sleep-time visuals, plots and dialogues might visit my brain for mutual dreams. Or they tell me something he wants me to know, maybe divulge what he doesn't want me to know. Sharing dreams may steal self-identity or could it help marriage merge in a good way.

Most people keep their individual uniqueness in community, friendships and marriage. We all exist in time and space, and sleeping beside one spouse for half a century must affect us. Couples share grunts and gurgles. We are privy to little sighs, and big cries of fear from the sleeping form next to us in bed.

When I awake in the morning and Ted's still sleeping, I like to look at his face. Unwrinkled, he looks young, almost baby-like. There's his knitted cap that he wears in cold weather to keep his bald head warm. Sometimes the nightcap is at a rakish angle and I almost laugh but he looks too peaceful to disturb. I wonder what he is dreaming.

Sleeping together means intimacies such as the mere presence of Ted's warm body next to mine. He says he's always cold, especially his feet but I find a warming radiation. Our postures resemble nestling silver spoons, or back to back. Heads rest on different-sized pillows. When I returned from my year in Japan, I continued to sleep on a small Japanese-style hard pillow stuffed with rice husks. Ted prefers his head twice as high as mine, yet our dreams could still mingle.

On an Amazon river-boat trip, in our old-fashioned cabin, Ted and I slept on built-in right-angled bunks. On the lower bunk, my feet lay under his head on the raised bunk. At Holden, in separate beds six feet apart, we faced physical estrangement, a sudden formality of distance.

That evening in our room, Ted described a re-run head-movie of his: "I'm taking a test and am completely unprepared. The questions on the exam mean nothing to me. I don't even know what course it is. The experience is frightening."

He continued: "And last night I dreamed that Jack-Tar wouldn't obey me. Our dog wouldn't even sit."

We talked about stormy nights at home when our outside dog slept on a pillow next to our bed. During the night we hear his muffled barks and whinnies of terror. His legs jerk and thrash. If only he could tell us what he dreams.

As Ted and I talked, I brushed my teeth at the little basin in our room, and gargled out these words. "Maybe we are not responsible for our dreams."

Ted unlaced his boots. "If we're not, who is?"

Putting away the brush, I looked at the ceiling for answers. Dreams do not lie and night dreams are more cohesive and sensible than day dreams. But do dreams enter the soul? Is life a butterfly's dream? Trying to decipher dreams made me feel like a midwife at a difficult birth. I put Tom's toothpaste away. My mind wandered in a semi-conscious state. "I don't know who is responsible for our dreams. Let's sleep on it."

Writers have described retreats for those needing help with their nocturnal dream-life. The "students" study lucidity and talk about "inner chambers of one's psyche." In a *New York Times* feature, words such as magic realm and ultimate human freedom described topics to be covered. Quotes included ancient Greeks and Tibetan monks who trained themselves to consider dream-life the same as waking life. Intrigued by the idea, I wondered if that was good or bad.

Over the centuries, there has been this argument about dreams, from "rubbish of the mind" (Nobel Laureate Francis Crick) to "dreams as messages generated by repressed energies" (Freud). Carl Jung said dreams "remind us of our wishes...are messages from ourselves to ourselves." Martin Luther dismissed the subject as "the work of the devil."

Others speak of dreams to gain greater knowledge, create a model of the world, or to play an influential role in cultural evolution. Our lives can imitate these dreams with personal creations of narratives and problem solving.

This dream stuff might help us with the Gnome and Witch, in a civilized way. Neighbors are "the test" for which we're unprepared; they are comic book characters driving a steam roller straight toward us. We are as helpless as the tramps, Estragon and Vladimir in *Waiting for Godot*. One of Samuel Beckett's characters tells the other he had a dream, but the other says,. "Don't tell me!"

The existential playwright lets Estragon plead his case with this question: "Who am I to tell my private nightmares to, if I can't tell them to you?"

Indeed. Ted wound the alarm clock, and reminded me: "First thing tomorrow for us, is *Garbology* Team at eight."

Holden's made-up name of Garbology and Ted's methodical scheduling, made me laugh and forget about dreams. Recycling garbage for a community of 400 smelled like a nightmare to me, no matter what name it wore.

At the stone wall behind the dining room, we gathered at 8:00 am with six other members of the day's Garbology team, mostly young men. Chief Garbologist, Sherm, sighed, sat down next to Ted and me on the wall, and proclaimed. "Garbology *is* ecology,"

He tucked his shirt into his jeans. "I've done Garbology for seven years. I'm leaving soon."

"What are you going to do then?" Ted asked.

"Sleep in." This rugged, strong man said his day begins at four in the morning. "Already today, before I came here, I collected all the garbage from yesterday, broke the glass, put it in used milk cartons to store them in an old school bus."

I had seen the buses up on the hill. "What eventually happens to it?"

"When several buses are full, I mean really packed, we drive them onto a barge, then off at the town of Chelan to a place that buys glass."

Sherm directed our crew of six to walk down the main street to the sorting shed where a huge wooden tray of trash awaited us. He urged us to put on gloves. I noticed he didn't wear any.

"Never did," Sherm explained. "When I asked the doctor last year about my not-wearing-gloves, he said he didn't see any disease I had picked up from the garbage. So I should have no problem."

Sherm raked through the plastic, metal, paper, cardboard, newspapers and magazines on the tray with his bare hands. He read a hand-written note, tossed it aside: "Not too interesting. Well, sometimes I find good stuff, or something like a *Sports Illustrated, Swimsuit Issue.*"

Our job began with separating burnable and compostable categories. Sherm twisted the top of each bag we filled and piled them in his truck. "I'm driving up to the incinerator and compost bins."

Incinerator! This was a garbology nightmare. Was it literal, metaphysical, moral or mystical?

" The rest of you will walk." Sherm added.

Some volunteers drew the line there. Becky, a 70-year-old volunteer, had told me at a chalet tea party, she couldn't walk up that hill and then shovel compost. "I just say I am too old to do Garbology and they say OK."

But Becky misses out. The intent behind Garbology is a beautiful one for the environment. Holden will not leave behind a big dump, or junk pile, the way the copper miners did. "A god-awful mess," is how Sierra Club's David Brower described Holden after hiking by the deserted mining town forty years ago. "It's the sort of place that gives mining a bad name... rusting old cars, junk, trash. That's what a mine does to wilderness."

In John McPhee's book *Encounters with the Arch Druid,* the author and Brower plus hikers of opposing viewpoints, argue about current standards of living vs. the beauty of mountain wilderness. One hiker proclaimed, "Ancient druids used to sacrifice human beings under the oak trees. Modern 'druids' worship trees, sacrifice human beings to the oaks."

In a similar vein, another hiker quoted important needs for copper. He argued that he would not "penalize people today for the future." Brower answered, "But I would."

So would I. Most humans ignore our ecology system. We will disappear from Earth, predicts E. O. Wilson, with no ill effects on the rest of life on this planet "except for pets and house plants." That puts us in our place, except workers like Sherm, and crusaders like David Brower.

When Ted and I belonged to the San Fernando Valley Bike Club, I had a similar conversation with a fellow bike rider who rode the bus to work, cutting down on smog. I said to him, "That's great. How far is the bus stop from your house?"

"One mile," he answered. "My wife drives me there."

"Drives you there!" I was stunned. Here was a serious biker who could cycle fifty or one hundred miles a day but wouldn't bike or walk one mile to the bus stop. Gathering my ideas together, I asked, "What's more important? The environment or your comfort?"

"My comfort." He answered quickly, looking proud about the rightness of his stand.

Defeated, I feared there were more like him than there were like David Brower. Doesn't anyone care about our grandchildren's grandchildren's world and everyone else's descendants, too? What about sustainability, and doing no harm?

Here we worked with Sherm and his Garbology team, who stood with David Brower. Sherm said everything goes back to the earth, provides nutrients for plants in the village. Current villagers will not leave a mountain of tailings, only steaming compost. Our rag-tag team walked up the hill to the incinerator, which looked like the one in my dream except for its big smokestack.

The huge door gaped while Sherm ignited the propane gas. Flames roared, turned the furnace into a sacred volcano pushing our team backwards into a lineup. Heated to the core, I relived my burning dream, adding ray-guns blasting their fireworks, and school buses charging out of nearby garages, spilling glass shards.

Sherm was calm at the Holden fire pit. Shoving metal trays filled with dozens of milk cartons packed with meat scraps, he propelled the garbage into the fire. It sputtered, crackled, consumed each offering. Our crew formed an assembly line to empty Sherm's truckload into the fire. When he slammed the furnace door, he said. "Now we do the composting."

Twenty compost bins held material in various states of readiness. On the ground, huge trays waited for the mixing of ashes, sawdust and fruit/vegetable scraps. Sherm opened a wooden box of kitchen and butcher knives.

"Citrus and banana peels have to be cut up. So do onions – you know, a whole rotten onion." He handed out the knives and boards, and added, "I've got band-aids."

A crew member, Jib, sliced his index finger while chopping orange peel in his bare hand. Bloody, bandaged, undaunted, the teenager continued mixing the compost tray. When we dispatched its contents into the bins, Sherm dismissed us from duty: "You've done a great job."

My daily efforts at home, a measly yogurt-container each day of composting scraps, paled in comparison. Still I loved the idea as each morning I would dig down my scraps and water the compost. Respectable work, it was, a Mother Teresa kind of thing.

Worn out from our Garbologizing, Ted and I let gravity pull us down, back to the village to start our day's real work. Quietly, we climbed our lodge steps to the second floor and stared at the empty flag holder. I could imagine a jagged black border that encased the word "Kazoom." signifying a comic daydream.

Dreaming, I have learned, is a good friend listening to the dreamer, or a surrender into feelings that need to surface. To heal or help us, the dreaming matters by its mere presence, with or without meanings. It increases our sensitivity. My dreams of mountains and meadows taste like spring water with a watermelon twist.

Gymnastics on a rope may never work for me, or Ted may be chronically unprepared for some big test. We might dream of congenial neighbors with a picket fence covered with climbing roses. Or we could go beyond the continent, past incidental and accidental human experience. We can question who we are, where we came from, and how we decide where to go next.

Even though I feel empathy for the beauty and hilarity of life, and dreams, some part of me wants to learn how to use a ray-gun for revenge. Another facet wants to offer up my weakness to turn garbage into goodness.

I Left My Heart At Holden's Compost Bin

(with apologies to San Francisco's cable cars and Tony Bennet)

I left my heart at Holden's compost bin
high on a hill, devoid of sin –
not like those gas-guzzlin' cars
bringin' smog halfway to the stars.

Uncut banana peals fill the air.
They don't care
but I'll wait there

at Holden's compost bin
above the tailings 'n' broken glass.
Stoves burn animal fat fast.

If you come back for Holden's compost
spread it 'round where it's needed most.

barbara marysdaughter

Chapter Sixteen
Keepsakes

If I must build a church…let it be in the wilderness out of nothing but nail-holes. Stanley Kunitz

Sunday mornings seem like a gift to me since leaving the Lutheran church fifteen years ago. When Holden's application asked for church affiliation, they received this white lie from me: *Between churches.* Holden honors different beliefs (a Muslim woman gave the vespers message the week before we arrived) but I didn't want to make an issue out of un-churched status.

Ted filled out his application the same way but he's in a different category. Scratch his non-membership status, and you will find a strong Lutheran family heritage. Still he was the one who initiated our break with the church over abortion rights.

Lutheran bishops, at their 1992 Florida convention voted that the U.S. Justice Department should decide if women could have abortions. When Ted heard that, he insisted we send a telegram to the convention. He had never reacted so sharply to a social issue before.

"What are we going to say?"

"They have no power to hand over women's rights," he answered.

Feminist writing had alerted me to the stifling womb-for-rent concept. Birthing decisions were women's business. Should petitioning women crawl on their knees before the U.S. Chief Justice?

We sent our don't-do-it message – like many other members – but the bishops did it anyway. This was not the Lutheran church we knew, marching in front of the civil-rights movement. After 40 years of active membership, I quit in protest. Ted couldn't go that far.

The weight of honoring deceased parents, grandparents and relatives still living in Minnesota and the Dakotas proved heavy for him. But Ted recognized my right to leave the church. Four years later we moved 200 miles north of Los Angeles and neither of us joined another congregation.

Ted misses the weekly rituals and socializing, drinking savory coffee and eating the sweets. At Holden he goes to vespers more than I do. Our community is asked to attend each evening but I go when I want to. A Jewish friend once asked me, "Do you believe all that stuff?"

"What stuff?" I had answered, ready to discuss, explain. Unfortunately, he didn't pursue the subject; I did, in the back of my mind for a decade or two. Holden's philosophy has room for my kind who are facing faults in the church but remembering its goodness. Would they accept my interest in ancient rites celebrated by Chumash women in my county? Would they call the Long Dance, where we women dance all night, a pagan rite?

The Holden application says it is "open to all people regardless of race, gender, age, religion, national origin, marital status, sexual orientation, or handicap." Although my beliefs don't have an official creed, I know I fit in there somewhere. Holden states a beautiful inclusiveness and I honor it in my way.

On Sunday mornings I am guided to the church of the great outdoors, looking through nail-holes as expressed by Poet Laureate Stanley Kunitz. Einstein said he believes in "Spinoza's God" personified as Nature. But Einstein expressed concern "whether God had any choice in creating the world."

At Holden I ran through the forest on Sunday mornings, often toward the ball field and labyrinth, alongside the creek. I dipped into near-wilderness and planned to sketch different views, unexplored by me so far.

This Sunday a fearless mother and her twin fauns stopped to stare at me on the bridge over Railroad Creek. The babies seemed unsure until I sat quietly on the opposite edge of the span. I drew bubbling creek water, my current challenge, while the deer grazed the bank behind me. No longer any challenges.

This is the creek Matt and I had hobbled by at the end of our hike. Now I had time to study its gurgling whirls and eddies rushing to the lake 12 miles away. Train track had been laid here 67 years ago to haul out copper, but that's as far as the project ever went: no train. My sketches of water weren't going anywhere either.

The deer ambled on and I put notebook and pencil in my pocket. Satisfied with our sharing this piece of creation, I ran back for breakfast. My aloneness helped me remember lines from a poem by my friend Kyoko Asano: *How Vast is Your Aloneness:*

…quiet knowingness…witnessing something of consequence…that God is alone…and there is nothing else…

A large, dark piece of bark on the ground caught my eye. It was shaped like a deer, running in the wilderness. I picked up the ten-inch-long keepsake and knew it would fit on our windowsill. This simple piece of "found art" looked like a caveman's, or cave woman's depiction of a wild animal. On our departure day, I would carry this piece of bark back into the woods behind our lodge where I often surprised grazing deer.

At dinnertime, Ted and I sat at a table with Roxanne, a wildflower expert, and her husband, a Lutheran pastor. "Gardener for the week," explained the friendly man, bearded with gray flecks in his hair. "I'm Roxanne's assistant, a wheelbarrow-pusher."

The couple had honeymooned at Holden thirty-two years before. "That's when I drew my first botanical sketch just up the hill." Roxanne shrugged her long blond hair out of the way and pointed out the window. "The plant was a columbine, *Aquilegia formosa*."

"You know the Latin names?" I asked.

"Only because," she answered, "I put my sketches together for a book on the wildflowers here."

After breakfast I bought her book at Holden's store, and read her words which sang out to me: "I was moved to tears when I first saw the alpine meadows...the pristine wilderness that I hope all can experience once in their lifetime."

The next day when we transplanted wildflowers together, Roxanne said she was sorry her children never had the chance to spend a whole summer working here. I told her that my kids and grandkids had been in the village for three days, just two weeks previous "and none of them wanted to stay any longer." We agreed that this "intentional life" does not appeal to everyone, or at every stage of one's life.

The six-foot-long wooden planter at the Village Center entrance looked like something used to pan gold or copper. Crammed with rhubarb plants, the huge flower box interested Roxanne: "The rhubarb has to go."

Nancy and I started yanking out the lush plants with their long healthy roots. Rhubarb grew all over the village but never appeared on the menu, or in the cookbook. No one knew why.

Roxanne continued, with a dreamy, determined voice: "This planter will be a showcase of Holden wildflowers, all name-tagged. Visitors will learn the names."

The fifty transplants that we had readied included trillium, cow parsnip, penstemon, firewood, lupine and yarrow. They waited in the shade. Roxanne's display could be a hallowed trophy case, a token from the wilds. The three of us began to clear the giant box of leaves, stalks and roots.

One of the old six-foot planks on the side of the huge box crumbled into dust. Pungent topsoil poured onto the sidewalk, forming a dune-shaped pile with a hothouse scent, a radiant sensation. "The rhubarb roots," Nancy wailed, "must have held it all together."

Roxanne's fair complexion turned red. "What to do! We're leaving tomorrow. I have to finish this today."

"We need a carpenter." Nancy made an executive decision.

Since both of our husbands were carpenters, only a block away, that seemed like the solution. Roxanne told us to clear out the remaining rhubarb while she went for help.

In minutes, she was walking toward us with Ted. He had his tape measure out to size up the situation. Roxanne was exuberant. "He is our shining knight on a white horse, coming to save the day."

"It's nothing." Ted shrugged off her compliments, wrote down dimensions, and checked the remaining boards. "They should last a couple of years."

He went to get the new plank. We gave the transplant natives some water. "How can these little weak plants survive 15 feet of snow?" I asked.

Roxanne smiled. "What do you think they do in the wilds?"

"Oh, yes," I conceded. "But will the name tags survive?"

She shrugged and we all agreed the quaint wooden box with its wild-flowers, right at the door to the Center, would be a success. But next to an empty flagpole holder? The stolen flags might still be missing but I could picture a brightly colored pennant from a distant country returned to its place, snapping in the wind.

Roxanne sounded exhilarated: "Ted said it was no big deal but I came up here to accomplish certain things and won't be back till next year. To me, his help is a saving grace. I'm going to praise Ted at the staff meeting tonight."

"He might be embarrassed," I said. "Say it anyway."

The lame joke: "I came here as a Lutheran and left as a lentil" originated as a tribute to the most popular dinner at Holden, lentil loaf. Maybe spinach squares are a close second, but lentil loaf is up there. This dinner emitted alluring scents of bay leaf, thyme and oregano. This would be our first chance to taste it.

Bright red bottles stood in rows at the kitchen serving window. The young woman next to Ted at the table told him, "We always eat lentil loaf with catsup."

He tried the combination. "Almost as good as my mother's meat-loaf."

Chewing on the textured loaf, I could savor carrots, onions, celery, maybe some wildflowers. At home I had cooked vegetarian loaves that were complete flops, like an avocado loaf that I try to forget. A good lentil loaf would be something else.

"Good without catsup," I decided, "and I want the recipe."

"It's in the Holden cookbook," said Rose, sitting across from us. "We sell them at the bookstore."

I had regular status there as a customer, checking for non-existent mail and purchasing literary keepsakes. The 62-page book, *Cook Boldly, with Care and Celebration* became mine and I wanted kitchen workers to autograph their favorite recipes.

But I was too late. Kitchen staff was off duty and dish team now prevailed. A dishwasher in his blue-rubberized apron said, "I'll put the book where they will see it."

The young man with soapy hands set my new cookbook down on the chopping block. I cringed. Everything looked clean, but I knew the kitchen's history: a work crew had taken thirty days to scrape away the kitchen grease from the mining days. That was then, of course. I left a note with my book for the kitchen staff to sign next to their favorite recipe.

After working again on planting the Village Center planter, I needed access to four windows off its second-floor balcony to plant flower boxes hanging outside. The plan called for overflowing flowers.

My boss, Jennifer gave me a tiny silver key on a string, for access to the rare off-limits, locked balcony area where it housed electronic sound equipment. "You can have the key."

With pride, I slipped the key-string around my neck. When it opened the fence-like door in the balcony, I felt trusted and responsible. Once inside the cloistered space, I pulled up the old-fashioned sash windows, leaned out and planted standard geraniums and petunias.

This second-story view fascinated me. Villagers scurried around on the brick sidewalks in a Find-Oswald cartoon-style, with plenty of color and action. At home, on the Central Coast of California, we could never see all our friends and acquaintances in one place like this, day after day. My plantings shouted out good feelings, too. Mother Teresa had said, if we want "love messages to be heard, they have to be sent out." Finished with my work, and study of the moving picture below, I stood up to close the windows.

Then I jumped a few inches off the floor. "Oh!"

Gary, the potter and sound engineer, switched on the electronic console. "Didn't mean to scare you. Just getting ready for the concert tonight."

Explaining to Gary why I had the key, I mopped up with the soles of my shoes, compost and water spilled on the floor, and asked about the concert.

"Three cellists," he said.

This gymnasium-turned-into-village-center and concert-hall, stood on our main street, a dirt road leading 11-miles through forest to the boat dock. Only two small towns, Chelan and Stehekin, existed on each end of the narrow, 50-mile long lake. The rest is wilderness.

"You're not kidding about three cellists here, are you?"

"Come and see."

Ted and I sat in the front row of the Village Center for an intimate theater-in-the-round setting. Three cellos, still in their cases, waited on stage. All three musicians were big women, appropriately sized for their instruments and the magnitude of this concert in the wilds of the Northern Cascades. One of the women had visited in the village before earlier. She had large hair, puffed out and gray, like a halo, and had completed her memorable image by carrying a carved staff.

To get here, the women had traveled five hours on the Lake Chelan boat, to be picked up by Holden's school bus for the 11-mile ride up the switchbacks. Guests of Holden, for the night plus all meals, the musicians offered us their best.

The women placed chairs and music stands so the audience on every side could see each one clearly. Confident and friendly, they announced their numbers to a hushed audience. A soft breeze wafted through the open doors. Alpine peaks surrounded us. We listened to the passionate tones of three cellos.

I caught my breath, inhaled harmonies these women offered us, forgetting names of composers, pieces or even performers. The audience floated on the vibrating notes from sacred and classical music to Appalachian folk. Everyone seemed intense and followed each lyrical sound. Between numbers, the women talked about the cello, their careers, where they had met each other, and how often they made music. These musical artists gave us one encore after another.

Keep the music, I repeated in my head. Keep the church music. It's too good to shun, to remove from my life. Never resign from the music with its passion, subtle harmonies, intricate chords. Resign from organized structure, creeds and restrictions if you must, but keep the music.

"A world is to be fought for, sung, and built." wrote American poet Muriel Rukeyser, "love must imagine the world." This community was still building and fighting for a world where love rules. The musicians at Holden sang it into reality. They carved it into the Village Center lectern with these words: *We Have the Treasure.*

In many diverse ways, our guests and volunteers find it. Ted and I wanted to hear and sing Marty Haugen's *Holden Evening Prayer* service. The composer had written his 12-page score while he lived with Holden's winter community, 1985-86. Ted and I then heard his hauntingly beautiful piece of music and words, the following summer. Written for counterpoint with leader, soloists, and congregation, the score contains repetitious lines that we find intimate and moving. The next evening's vespers emerged itself in Haugen's service:

> *God of mercy*
> *hold us in love*
> *help us*
> *comfort us*
> *all of our days*
> *keep us*
> *hold us*
> *spirit of love*
> *be our guide and path*
> *for all of our days*

How does a God of mercy hold us in love? Did it matter that I didn't know? I stretched the concept that "us" meant me, Ted, our children, grandchildren and friends. Aren't there more? Is that all of "us?" Then I bumped into our sociopath neighbors and was afraid to continue.

But yes, they are included: Gnome and Witch, who have placed by our fence line, deep in the woods at home, a stake that contains the Bible verse, "If God is with us, who can be against us?" in its entirety. Should we place a tape of Haugen's music on our side of the fence? Who owns this God of mercy? Who divides neighbors into *us* and *them*?

We bought a copy of Haugen's liturgical music at the bookstore. Score and words suited each other, words insisted on repeating themselves. Hypnotized by the repetition, we wallowed in the counter-point, round-like overlays, such as *hold us in love, hold us in love, comfort us all of our days.*

Keep the music, I told myself again, and keep the wisdom in the teachings. Apply good concepts to universal citizenship, stretch them over our country's foreign policy, and back to the neighbor whose lies sent Ted to jail. Remember that turning the other cheek is broad-enough for non-violent diplomacy and narrow enough to fit our easement.

Yet the reality of Ted's arrest, only six weeks previous, woke me from my reverie of how things should be. A new friend at Holden gave me a quote from a "citizen of Rome," as she described him: " a neighbor is 'to hate.'"

Neither she nor I agreed with that Roman citizen. We are *them* and they are *us*. But we might concede that some neighbors ask to be hated.

The next morning I picked up my autographed cookbook, signed by 11 kitchen workers. Marsha had written her name next to the Agg-kaka recipe (a Scandinavian breakfast dish): *Excellent! I know it sounds strange but it's great.* Kristian wrote: *I love Holden bread.* Katie K. signed by the Lentil Loaf recipe: *The best.* No one autographed Baked Eggs Florentine, "Breakfast for 449 close friends" which calls for 650 eggs.

Some red sauce smeared the title page of my book but that seemed relevant once I caught its scent. The philosophy expressed in the cook book includes who grows the food, buys it, cooks it, eats it, and scrapes the scraps into the compost bin. Love and fervor for sustainability of the earth, this autographed-keepsake cookbook is dedicated to *those who dare to eat boldly.*

I had to confess boldly to Jennifer that I had lost the little silver key to the balcony. "I don't know," I wailed, "what happened to it."

"I can get you another one." she said.

Who would find that key and steal the valuable electronic equipment protected by its lock? Yet no one expects a thief in this village. We are a trusted, and trusting community, most of the time. At dinner, a glowing Dianne announced that the flags had been found.

Villagers probably remembered Dianne's plea when the flags disappeared and her promise of anonymity and no punishment when returned. Hoorays and cheers erupted all over the dining room but quickly quieted down to hear the details: "Some hikers saw this pile of colorful material on the ball field, and brought the flags to our office. The flags are tattered, dusty, dirty and ripped. Volunteers in the laundry will wash and mend them. They will fly again in a few days."

Found in the ball field, next to the labyrinth with its spiritual powers, the lost flags might have been found by the angels of the ball field. Or of the wilderness! Maybe, angels hang out in the mountains or so I would like to think. Satisfied and relieved, I didn't turn around, to look for guilty faces in the dining room.

Lentil Loaf

(AUTOGRAPHED Aug. 2002: *It's lentil loaf. It's good
for you. Just use a little ketchup. You'll get that lentil loaf down! Libby
The Best! Katie K.*)

2 ½ C dry lentils
3 C cooked rice
3/4 C pecans or walnuts, toasted and chopped
2 eggs, beaten (optional)
1 onion, chopped
1 C carrots, diced or grated
1 C celery, chopped
2 ½ C bread crumbs
½ C olive oil
2 ½ tsp chili powder
1/4 tsp cayenne
2 tsp dry mustard
3 tsp garlic powder
1 tsp thyme
ketchup

Method: Boil lentils in water until soft, about 30 minutes. Drain and combine with the remaining ingredients. Season to taste. Add enough ketchup to achieve a thick paste, but not enough to overpower spices. Place in greased bread pan and bake at 350 degrees for 50 to 60 minutes. Let set for 5 minutes before slicing.

Option: This recipe makes a mild loaf. Add more spices according to your taste. Many people like adding mushrooms, too! Serve with additional ketchup on the side.

Chapter Seventeen
Labyrinth Is a Pilgrimage

The labyrinth connects us to the depths of our souls so we can remember who we are.
Lauren Artress, Pastor at Grace Cathedral, San Francisco;
founder of Verditas Worldwide Labyrinth Project

A woman I know, blind in one eye, completed a 450-mile hiking pilgrimage from the Pyrenees in France to Santiago de Compostela in Spain. "And I'm not even Catholic," she said, "but at the end I experienced a revelation. I learned how it all works."

Radiant and smiling, she said she understood the universe and her place in creation. "For a short time, I even knew who I was," she added. "But since I didn't write it all down I forgot what my revelation was."

Didn't remember! Forgot her revelation! Amazing to me, but at the same time, I understood. Some things seem so right they blend into the marrow of our bones, and they're there whenever needed. We don't record them and sometimes we can't recall them ever again.

Did her forgetting make the trek a failure? Not at all, she argues. She regained the sight in her eye, but insists that the "real grace" is in the journey itself.

Prospective pilgrims long to prepare for, as well as visit, the sacred place that calls to them. The getting ready is a blessed activity. They exalt in the adventure of getting there, even though half of them quit and never make it. Some die along the way from exposure, malnutrition or accidents.

For centuries, pilgrims have walked in the ancient dust of these paths. Reasons for pilgrimages range from questioning life's purpose to preparing for death. Many pilgrims don't know why they go. An omen, or just a few words at their quest brings them satisfaction.

In many ways, my family's glacier climb and trek through the wilderness was a pilgrimage to Holden, often called "a place apart." Three days with nature's wildness and stormy uncertainty brought out unexpected strength for us to pull through. We accepted a challenge that healed something inside to make us closer to each other than before. Although our paths took many turns, we never faltered in a tricky maze. Our complex hiking trails shepherded us labyrinth-like, switch-backed us to the goal.

Before our trip to Holden, I had dipped my toe in labyrinths, starting with Grace Episcopal Cathedral on Nob Hill in San Francisco. A replicate of the world's most famous labyrinth at France's Chartres Cathedral, this 100-ft. diameter, 11-circuit design dominates its traditionally-correct church-foyer location at Grace. Pastor Lauren Artress wrote the 1995 book that kicked off the "rediscovering of the labyrinth as a spiritual tool," and she helped create both indoor and outdoor versions of this labyrinth.

With two hiking friends of mine, we three women had burst through the cathedral's heavy carved doors into its spacious sanctuary. Beamed ceilings soared to the heavens. I spotted the sign "Remove shoes to walk Labyrinth."

Taking off my boots, I lined them up with shoes belonging to three labyrinth walkers who moved in the midst of their roundabout process. My friends expressed more interest in the gift shop and ladies room. I wailed, "You don't want to try this?"

"Not really."

"Go ahead. We'll wait for you."

It was my first labyrinth and it called to me. Why not to them? I had no instructions, no orientation. I watched the three experienced walkers out there, moving slowly. Their eyes focused on the warren of paths. I started, wondering what I should think and do. The walkers ahead would be my teachers. I watched them with the eye of an apprentice.

Intricate paths reminded me of an electronic circuit board, or sheet music distorted and curved by a copy machine. Or it mimicked a diagram of my brain. This path even recalled nightly water-picking of my teeth: follow the top-row curve in front, make a U-turn and do the concave inner side.

My mind wandered to its depths as my feet massaged the tile floor, through my hiking socks. I might even sink through to the earth underneath with its intricate tree roots, cleft rocks and sand. Then my feet could imprint heel, arched instep, and toes on top of footprints of earlier walkers.

But my friends waited on the bench for me; I knew I couldn't dawdle and increased my speed to reach the center and retrace my steps. My meditative walk, introduction to the labyrinth, rushed to a close.

My next labyrinth awaited close to home in Avila Beach, with preparation provided. The Labyrinth Director of Sycamore Springs resort, in her trendy leisure suit, spoke to our group with authority. "Select a stone from the pile near the entrance to our outdoor labyrinth. Put whatever concerns, dilemmas, problems you have into that stone. When you arrive at the center, leave both your burden and the stone."

I dumped my ongoing neighbor-dilemma onto a flat stone, lightly striped in black and gray. My fingers pretended to carve the word *harassment* on the top of the stone. Stamped on top of that, *Miserable life* in white letters sparkled in the sun and in my imagination. Instantly, the edge of my other hand wanted to crush the stone like a Karate black-belt expert would do. Instead, feeling light-headed and buoyant on my feet, I cradled the stone. Paths leading to the center would tell us what to do. Twenty women walked the circles with me.

My friend Betty arrived at the center before I did. She threw her stone into the large, central circular clearing, with the force of a baseball pitcher. Betty's delivery of her rock was abrupt, an unexpected drama in this quiet scene. She looked as stunned as the rest of us.

Everyone stopped walking, meditating, adjusting their socks, examining the stones, whatever they were doing. We watched Betty's stone skip and bounce up onto the leg of another labyrinth walker.

"I'm so sorry," Betty cried out.

"It's OK. It's nothing," the woman answered.

The bare stone with its secret message settled into the raked dirt at the center. Quietness descended. The unruly, skipping stone seemed forgotten. I set down my stone and felt relief but no unconditional love for my tormentors. After all, the Gnome might still convince a deputy to arrest me.

I reversed direction and hurried back over familiar ground, thinking about my problem left behind with Betty's and a dozen or so other stones placed by the women. In some ways, we had shared "deep things" with each other by walking the labyrinth together.

The path looked different in reverse. My eyelids nearly closed from drowsiness but I never faltered. Noting some of my faster co-walkers gathered on benches in the shade, I joined them when I finished. Betty apologized again to the group.

The director answered, "I admire you for releasing your burden so physically, with such genuine emotion."

Two months later I faced the promise of Holden's labyrinth. With seven other women, I gathered in Creekside Room with Eunie Schroeder, our leader from Portland, Oregon. The tall, blond, young woman held degrees in spiritual care, and in the history and meaning of these circuitous paths. It surprised me that one could get a Master's degree in labyrinths.

"These designs exist in prehistoric cave drawings in Europe," Eunie told us. "Hopi Indians include the same meandering design in their Mother-Earth art. Ancient Hebrew stones have these intricate-circle designs carved into them. And the oldest, seven-circuit/single pathway labyrinths date from 3500 BC."

Eunie gave us local background. "Volunteers worked on Holden's 11-circuit, 100-foot diameter labyrinth as soon as the snow melted the previous winter. They raked, laid out the design, added chipped bark and lined paths with stones from Railroad Creek."

That was close to the Ball field that Matt and I had struggled by a few weeks earlier, to the applause of angels. Had the angels just finished walking the labyrinth?

Our expert emphasized the difference between maze and labyrinth. "A maze leads you astray with choices, sends you around a wrong turn. You end up in a dead end. In a labyrinth, you'll never get lost, or trapped, for you always end up at the center."

"How do you get out?" asked a women in the class.

"Retrace your steps. Turn around and go back."

Another woman from Portland asked, "What do you do when you reach the center?"

"That's up to you," answered Eunie. "Some stand or sit to meditate. If you're alone, lie down, stay as long as you like."

I thought about Betty's hurled stone and wished she could come to Holden. The rest of this group picked up on possibilities for center-actions: You could sing, suggested one. Pray out loud, said another. Kneel. Dance. Our group looked eager and ready to have a soles-on experience with the labyrinth. Energy in the room whirled, bounced off the corners and enveloped our leader. She put down her chalk. "Are you ready?"

We sprang out of our chairs and followed her down the deserted dirt road, left the village behind, headed for wilderness. Empowered to see clearly, we walked with great energy to live well, love well and be open to the labyrinth. We asked more questions.

"Should we walk it really slow?"

"What if we want to pass someone?"

"If we're tired can we step over a line for a shortcut?"

"Do we greet someone coming the other way?"

"What if we kick a stone out of place?"

Our tireless leader answered: "Go at the right pace for you but make it steady and rhythmic. Stretch your bodies, minds, and ideas. It's OK to pass. If tired, take a rest. There's no time limit and no shortcuts. You could greet people with a smile but don't step over a line and please, replace all disturbed stones."

"You know," said a black teenager in our group, a kitchen volunteer, "I've been shredding cabbage all morning, and the pattern inside a cabbage head is like a labyrinth."

Eunie nodded. Yes, I thought, and it's also like the cow paths on our hills at home, or the way kids get lost in cornfields, or it's a side-view of a cinnamon roll.

The kitchen-worker's mother told me they were from Australia where there is a saying "that the labyrinth is what the earth has to tell us."

Couldn't I get that message from the earth, here on this dirt road? Do I have to go into some altered-mind state? Did I need a revelation to find out how it all works? Must I call on God, or Jesus, the Holy Spirit, or some specific saint?

Our group turned off the road at the meadow where low fog floated toward the surrounding trees. Two deer bounded away. All was quiet. Weak sun rays spotlighted the tansy flowers springing up between the paths. These invasive yellow daisies kill native flowers. Maybe we should throw stones at them.

If the tansy is an evil invader of native-plant turf, then I need to deal with evil. Was the earth of this labyrinth telling me that? Or, was the message that the tansy, like the Gnome and Witch, are all part of creation? And that native plants and invasive plants can not live together in peace.

"We'll gather back at this bench when we're through," Eunie said, "and talk about our experience." She suggested we line up, and allow ten seconds between our starts. "Bow your head if you like, or hold your hands in a prayer position. You can say 'Namaste'."

"What does that mean?" asked one of the quiet members of our group.

"'I bow to the divine in you,'" said our leader. "Or to the inner life of all living things."

All living things include tansies. Picking one as talisman for my pilgrimage, I was third to go. With my focus on the path, I slowly arrived at that first right turn. Two walked ahead of me, nearing the center, but still in the first quarter. Our journey of turns had just begun and I suspected that the woman behind me wanted to pass. Labyrinth is life; you follow, pass, or knock pilgrims off the path, according to an ancient saying.

The woman passed peacefully. I recalled that a man had told me he repeated the Rosary when he walked the circuits. Another sharp turn advanced me into the second quarter. My tansy flower-head traveled in a tiny, velvet drawstring bag given to me by the woman who did the Spanish cathedral pilgrimage. Eunie had called the labyrinth a metaphor for life as we surrender ourselves to the path: "It's kind of like God; we don't know why it works."

Neither did 17th-century philosopher Gottfried Wilhelm Leibniz, inventor of calculus. In Paris when in his twenties, he had found mathematical ideas at one end of "the continuum of the labyrinth," biographer Matthew Stewart wrote. On the other end, Leibniz envisioned "nothing but an infinite number of point-like, immortal souls."

In my imagination, Ted seemed to be with me on this labyrinth walk. We are newly weds, 50 years younger and I am about to join the Lutheran church, his family's tradition. I have to be re-baptized; my Unitarian naming ceremony doesn't count. I had always wanted to be like my friends who were baptized as babies, went to confirmation class, and studied the Bible. But to be christened at age 23 seemed bizarre.

"I'll need to wear a little white bonnet and a long dress," I said to my new husband as I floated on the circuits, giggling, crying in a mindful re-run of being ashamed to live 23 years un-baptized. I wanted acceptance by church and members. This event became bigger than a formality. My parents weren't invited to my christening for fear they might be hurt that their "naming" of me at the Unitarian church wasn't considered good enough. All of that came back on this labyrinth walk. Did I know who I really was when I was baptized? Do I know who I am fifty years later?

More paths to follow. Other pilgrims dawdled; I strode onward, hardly slowing down for U-turns. The earth inquired about the word intentional. Was I doing this walk with a purpose, a plan? Being whomever I intended to be? Does the mind fit the labyrinth (to paraphrase author Annie Dillard) and shape it as a river shapes its own banks? My mind wandered to neighbors, Gnome and Witch, who act like intentional people – with purpose, plan, goal.

Stepping along the familiar path, I found ideas bombarding me. Unconditional love insists that neighbors can be whomever they happen to be. I imagined the Witch watering Holden's baby grass, and the Gnome building shelves next to Ted in the carpentry shop, and helping with the cement-finishing team. Both of them go to vespers with us, walk the labyrinth.

In my stupor, I fantasize a Sicilian, raised in the "cradle of vendetta" as Laura Blumenfeld wrote in her book *Revenge*. Two Palestinians, lifted from the pages of her book, walked this path to assure all of us that their shootings were nothing personal: "It was just some Jew!" The mother of the shooter caught up with me, in my day dream, slapped me on my thigh and whispered, "The family was with him. It was for the honor of our people."

At the center of the labyrinth, I stood for a few moments to clear my mind and wanted to laugh but felt gagged by propriety. It was like the time Judy (as a teenager) and I giggled at a do-unto-others communion service. The chunk of bread she tried to fit into my mouth proved too big. We collapsed in uncontrollable laughter. Afterwards, fellow parishioners said they liked our giggles.

Laughter goes with the whole business of labyrinth, not in derision but joy in playing with its circular pathways and one's imagination. Walking in circles does that. The nearby gurgle of rushing creek waters reminded me of the deer, just minutes ago. Do bears ever walk these paths?

Labyrinth is life, with the center as attainment, or goal. My mind escaped to that other path, the trail that leads out to Hart and Lyman lakes and the glaciers. In a backward re-run, our family treks in reverse, climbs up the snowfield, slides down Spider Glacier to Larch Knob campsite. I bound across the logjam bridge, saunter through the meadow's wild flowers and see no tansies blooming there. The fat mountaineer receives thanks for his good advice. The parking-lot bulletin board displays my report: Climbing Spider Glacier led me to a labyrinth that picked my brains, mended my mind, and bonded me with an invasive exotic.

Instantly Ted is back with me in the center of the labyrinth. He says his heels don't hurt anymore and we can walk the circuits together in my fantasy.

"There's beauty in this mathematical diagram," he says. "The paths are like a graph." Arms around each other's waist, we begin the walk-out together, side by side until Ted disappears.

The trip back on the path seemed familiar but different in a special way. I remembered who I was on my trip in and felt changed. Part of my life had flashed before my mind-screen and I pictured the harassing neighbors as invasive exotics, like the tansy.

Gathering at the bench to share experiences, Shirley, the potter, told us she particularly noted the 90-degree turns for each quarter. Another walker saw exciting parallels with her recent chance to swim with dolphins. Others called out these impressions:

"It's a mirror, reflecting back what I need."

"A chance to explore the journey of my life."

"Next time I will go barefoot."

We straggled back on the road to the village, together but spread out, separate and in our own heads but still bonded. My life had trapped me at times in a maze, with too-many choices, some dead ends. Inhaling the group's positive energy, I wanted to follow the labyrinth pattern to solve problems. I touched my talisman, good-luck charm, tansy-head outcast. Next, I needed to carry it to the special bin for invasive plants. I would throw no stones at it.

Ted had decided not to go to vespers that night, although we had walked over to the Village Center together. "I'm too tired," he said. "But you could go."

"OK, but I'll sit near the door so I can leave early if I want to."

Picking up a hymnal, I chose to join a group sitting on the floor, leaning against the wall near the door. Mai, the woman in the college group from Kyushu, was next to me. She smiled when I sat down. When singing began, she shared my songbook. Her soprano voice sounded flute-like as she held her side of the book and I gripped the other. Our voices together gave me peace, inner gratitude and inner health. A connection to the Japanese group blossomed through Mai, the only one attending vespers. She told me they were all leaving the next day on the early bus.

"I'll be there to wave you on your way home," I promised.

In time to see the group boarding the bus, I recognized Mai although she was crying. Tears streaked her beautiful, vulnerable face. When she turned for one last token look at the people, and the Village, she saw me. She smiled like a sunrise and waved. The door shut and the bus pulled away.

Japanese students leaned out of the windows, waving their signals of farewell. About ten of us wavers kept our arms going. The bus advanced into the shade of the trees by the schoolhouse, then out into a pocket of sun. The students' waves flourished with energy. We all kept our arms up, throbbing and wavering. When the bus disappeared in the next dark, shady spot of the road to turn a corner, we put our tired arms down.

"That's so Japanese," I said, to anyone around who wanted to listen.

"No, it isn't," said a woman I hadn't seen since the waving-off of our own family, weeks ago. "It's Scandinavian."

The near-by post office window attracted me. Ted and I had not heard anything from our family but the woman in charge called out to me: "There's a package for you."

"Really?" I felt like a character in a play at a turning point in the drama.

"See?" She produced a square brown-paper wrapped box, with Judy's return address.

Moving out to a bench on the small roofed porch, I unwrapped the package as Val, our Lodge One neighbor walked by.

"Lucky you." She watched me unveil a photo album, about nine by seven, that Judy had made. On the cover was a photo of me struggling to get out of the tent. My nose and the nose of my boot protruded through the not-quite unzipped entry way. The back cover featured a photo of me tightening my backpack's belly-band. I had stuck my tongue out to show the agony of it all.

Dave, the head waitri, came by on his way to work. "Hi, did someone get mail?"

I showed him some of the glacier pictures, in startling black and white. Both he and Val, wife of Jerry the ice cream manager, became enthusiastic.

"Jerry would love to see these."

We agreed to meet before dinner on the deck at The Ark for show-and-tell. I headed for the carpentry shop to share the glow with Ted.

Cinnamon Rolls

(AUTOGRAPHED Aug. 2002; *I LOVE cinnamon rolls!*
Laura Johnson)

Dough:
2 tsp yeast
1/4 C warm water
½ C sugar
½ C margarine or shortening
2/3 C milk
2 eggs
3 1/4 C white flour

Filling:
½ C margarine
1 C brown sugar
1 C white sugar
1 TBSP cinnamon

METHOD: Dissolve yeast in warm water. In separate bowl, beat sugar and margarine. Add milk and eggs. Slowly add yeast and flour, mixing until a moist, soft dough is formed. Knead for one minute (working dough too much will make it difficult to form). Cover dough with plastic wrap and a towel. Let rise in warm place for 45 minutes.

While dough is rising, melt margarine for filling. In a separate bowl, combine brown sugar, white sugar and cinnamon (include walnuts, raisins or any other addition you might like).

When dough has risen, knead it and roll into a rectangle. Brush surface with melted margarine and sprinkle filling on top so that it covers all the dough. Roll the dough up the long way, and pinch the edge of the body to form a seam. Cut pieces from the roll about 1" wide. Place on greased pan 1/4" apart.

Bake at 350 degrees for 20-30 minutes. Let sit 5-10 minutes before serving.

Chapter Eighteen
What We Casualy Call Violence

*Overcome oppression and violence without resorting to oppression
and violence.*
   Martin Luther King speech accepting Nobel Peace Prize, 1964

After enjoying another Death-by-Chocolate ice cream cone with
Ted, I hurried to a new class: *Violence in the Liturgy.* Would this be about
killing, torture and brutality in the name of religion? This heavy subject
contrasted with our day of gentle breezes, and blue skies crowding ever-
present alpine peaks.

But the subject reminded me of holy pictures on the walls of my
relatives. One at my great-aunt Barbara's showed Christ's heart outside
of his chest, bright red, with droplets of blood falling to the floor. The
image had frightened me but I didn't think of it as violent, so much as
accepting it as part of her religion. In a service hymnal, I once counted
fifteen hymns about Christ's blood. Bleeding belonged with these beliefs,
not mine.

Once again I wondered if the church hierarchy, back in their offices
in the Mid-West knew what we, in this wilderness, hashed over like
charging wildebeests. Squaring my shoulders, I stood up straighter. *Why
shouldn't we talk about liturgy violence?* At Holden we could talk about
anything. I joined the people crowding into the Fireside Room. Who
would guess these villagers in their bright colors, shorts and sandals were
interested in uncontrolled, intense and violent force?

Leading the class was a young woman, obviously pregnant. Mary, with
hair pulled back to show her pretty face, said she and her husband lived
in Chelan while she worked on her Ph.D. in theology. Our no-nonsense
teacher didn't mention their heir-apparent, being nurtured by her body.
Instead, she asked our group of 30, "Can you think of references to violence or physical abuse in hymns, doctrine, or liturgy?"

Mary held up her chalk to capture answers which came forth: precious
blood, crown of thorns, pierced side. The man next to me, sandals off,
shouted, "Fire and brimstone."

A woman, looking like the president of the Ladies Aid with her
upsweep hairdo, called out: "A fountain filled with blood." There were
favorites suggested like "The old rugged cross stained with blood divine."
And from communion liturgy came quiet remembrances: "Christ has...
become obedient unto death, even the death of the cross," and "the body

of our Lord Jesus Christ and his precious Blood." That one reminded me of my great-aunt's picture.

Never had I examined this idea, that church doctrine encouraged bloody gore. I had thought of Christianity as a peace-on-earth kind of religion: turn the other cheek and love your enemies. Jesus held daring and progressive views about peacemaking and stood for justice, equality, economic fairness, social programs and human rights. Therefore I believed the support of war and militarism became a misuse of spirituality.

A Scottish Episcopal pastor, Michael Easter, claims that Christians began as pacifists, with a fish as their symbol. Not until the fifth century did the cross begin to appear prominently in Christian art. Many paintings showed a crucified Christ; by the Middle Ages a tortured Christ.

"Then out marched the Papal army, and Crusaders roughed up the heretics," adds the Scottish pastor. "Americans became the most violent of all, a trait that harked back to their historic near-extermination of Native Indians."

Such strong statements. Why had I not heard them before? In Sunday-School adult discussion groups or in college gatherings? Ridiculous questions, I realized, remembering only bridge games at the student center and gossip in my sorority room.

But I did remember that Greek Gods like Neptune practiced rough, injurious discipline. I began to see where this class was going. Mass killings exist in the Old Testament, plus the Passover slaughter, plagues sent by God, and his directives in Samuel 15:3: *Go and attack the Amelakites and completely destroy everything they have. Don't leave a thing; kill all the men, women, children and babies; the cattle, sheep, camels and donkeys.*

In spite of my varied church experiences, I hadn't noticed this violent mayhem mentioned in the services, council meetings or church camps. But I wasn't always paying attention. Neither did I take rituals seriously, nor ask questions. I was afraid to reveal to the pastor or congregation that I had never read the Bible, and didn't think our family owned one. It took years of study, teaching Sunday School, and taking my turn on the council before I reached the point, described by F. Scott Peck, where "I wondered what they were *not* telling me." Now I question who were *they?*

Drawn to Native American Indians who lived on the Central Coast of California for 10,000 years, I began to meet them and learn about practices such as the Long Dance. One September, I spent time with the Sisters of the Dance, a weekend of work and ritual with peaceful women.

We built a sweat-lodge skeleton with supple willow saplings, tying them together with string made from jute. Precision ruled with our "sister" construction boss, now crippled with a bad leg. But Sky Rider showed her sisters how to wrap and tie each of the twenty poles, and fortify them into the earth with circling kindling sticks.

With graceful curves, this willow skeleton formed a low roof, hinting at final covering of blankets and rugs. A low entrance-door, less than three feet high, anticipated our crawling in – shoeless and, for some, naked.

We forty women gathered at dusk, covered by towel, sarong, robe or, in my case, silky thermals which I planned to remove when too hot. Shoes off, I crawled like a baby into the dark cavity and found my spot on the third tier, with a willow-limb-strut backrest. I watched, in the doorway's low light, women on all fours entering this womb, like animals loaded onto a truck. But I already knew I was an animal.

Advice from sweat-leader: remove pierced-ear earrings to avoid burned ears. Menstruating women, she said, are welcome in this sweat lodge. Then we prayed individually and together: words, requests, blessings, thanks – on top of another's prayer for symphonic chords and sounds like locusts or frogs. Deep darkness invaded when the door closed on us.

Our two fire-tenders aggressively opened that little door so that a stream of light greeted us. One woman handled the door and the other lifted a shovel carrying an ancient hot rock, the first of ten, for the fire pit. Both fire-tenders sang out a woeful greeting that sounded like: "Ohh-hhhhhhhhhhh, Mystafelees..."

Next came a pail of water, dumped over the hot rock, a ritual to be repeated until ten rocks are placed and the temperature rises to its highest level. We sweated, removed clothing, saw naked bodies when light came from the opened door. We sang songs. Each time the fire tenders came, we saw the steam, and felt a wave of new, intense heat, hotter than before. Four or five sisters left us when door opened; one came back. I thought it was just like biking through the dessert in July: peaceful and gratifying but making me sweat by the gallons. My mind went back to Holden Village.

"Why does religion need violence?" asked Mary, our scholarly teacher at Holden. "Why do Christians wear crosses, even crucifixes, instead of blades of grass?"

Fascinated by the blade-of-grass religious symbol, I wanted more on that. But the class raced on to reasons for violence: Classmates said it was to capture our attention like movie car-chases and barroom brawls;

violence echoes real life, threatens backsliders, keeps members on the right path, and increases membership.

Mary, the energetic mother-to-be, asked more questions than I could bring up: "Are we saved by violence? Redeemed by Christ's suffering and death?"

This class should have been meeting in the sauna or sweat lodge, with heat to sweat out the subject. A Finnish sauna or Japanese hot bath could have produced a casual atmosphere of benches, towels, crackling fire. Then we could stop to ponder these words and radical ideas from Mary's class, work with this new material. Holy-heat lethargy would slow us down so we can ask: why do humans need to be saved?

In the opera based on Goethe's Faust, salvation appears simple. Margarita, in spite of cavorting with Faust, learns she is saved when the word comes down from two chorus members on the backstage catwalk. The vanquished Devil, who predicted she was doomed, falls down in agony. This scene makes great theatre accompanied by beautiful music, but I want to know what Goethe and the audiences of that day really thought about original sin and redemption.

A church choir once barred a woman friend of mine from singing with them because she didn't believe in original sin. Most church members, I would bet, could not even explain the concept. Oh, they've heard about Eve and the apple but never really considered the meaning of original sin, and neither have I. In the sauna or a Chumash sweat lodge, we could mull these things over for 20 or 30 minutes, and see what we find. Redemption could be a metaphor for a loving life, at one with nature, or it might be a controlling legend used by religious leaders for more obedient parishioners.

"Does religious violence turn us into fanatics?" Mary continued, in our class in the Fireside Room. She quoted theologian Rebecca Parker who had written this story: Two students believe a gay young man they know is disobeying the Bible. They tie him to a fence and torment him. Eventually they beat him to death, calling their deed "God's work."

The answer to Mary's question – does religious violence turn some people into fanatics – is yes. Or is it the other way around: fanatics join groups that practice religious violence?

When Mel Gibson's film, The Passion of Christ came out, its graphic crucifixion scenes upset critics. Gregory Wolfe, writing in a Chesterton Institute for Faith & Culture publication, says Gibson's "sustained, graphic violence" shows a "resurgence of some sort of dark atavistic religion." This level of violence, he says, "turns Jesus into the gold medallist in the Olympics of Suffering."

Scholar Stephen Prothro criticized Gibson's "blood and guts sacramentality." Gregory Wolfe argues, "What other kind of sacrament is there? If God cannot become present in blood, guts, shit, piss, semen, saliva – he vanishes into the ether."

Prolific writer Joyce Carol Oates writes about blood ties, blood on the sheets, running though veins, and more. She shows blood to be the basic sign of life and brutal death. What would Mary say? Should we be thinking that no violence equals no God? Or, turned around: No God means no violence. Johan Galtung, former draft-resister, founder of International Peace Research in Oslo, told the 1994 UNESCO conference that "every religion in varying degrees has elements of the soft (towards peace), and hard (towards war)." He suggested "dialogue to strengthen the peace potentials."

And peace prevailed with Chumash Sisters of the Dance who gather together to learn about the Long Dance. Almost 100 of us, we heard that we needed to dance like it's our last dance because dance teaches. We needed intention. Since it had taken me three years to make time for this all-night celebration, I couldn't imagine not dancing as much as possible. But veterans of the Long dance said there are always some who spend a lot of time resting, eating, talking, sleeping. I became determined to dance all night. Curious as to what kind of dance step to do, I waited to see how others danced.

Clockwise! To the beat of six drummers on two large drums. who begin the rhythm with great force on their long-handled sticks. Drama is in the air. We pour into the circular dance floor (raked dirt). Some, alone like me, others in lines threaded together by hugging arms. I am behind such a group, recognize Buzzing Bear (volunteer for the Grandmother lodge) and decide I could join their threesome. A liveliness hits me, tells me this is my Long Dance at last. Invigorated by the beat, the acceptance of these three dancers – and there's another dancer on my left. I ask, "Want to join us?" She does.

Sisters of the Dance, all five of us spin on our way, accenting the drumbeat. At the drum-lodge platform, we stop to breathe in their rhythm, admire the women drummers. I am stunned to see Tybet whose tent stands next to mine in the campground. Such a smile on her face as she confidently hammers the rhythm. Afterwards, she tells me, "I really like drumming. I don't know why. You should try it."

The fifty-foot-circumference, sacred dance circle features one entrance-arbor that faces the rising-sun East: its opposite exit-portal, splendid with banner and flowers, leads dancers westward. We all must use these exits, and not walk over the berm of sculptured curling fingers of dirt surrounding the dance circle. That would break its spell, I was told when I forgot and trampled the berm.

More advice: "Dance on your knees to talk to the earth." "This dance circle is like a large womb of a mother." "Our song leader is a good teacher."

Later I answer the call for a drummer, and sing along with the song leader, with Tybet's big smile on my face this time. I rest in the Grandmother's lodge to study inside architecture of the tepees. The Moon Lodge for young women still menstruating, has eighteen poles with eighteen prayers wrapped in black ribbons near the top of each pole. Square knots in each knob of ribbon hold a written prayer from a sister of the dance. Streamers dance in the cooling winds.

Each tepee is skinned with decorated covers, precisely hung on the poles to reach from ground level to "gathering of pole tops." Opened wings of ventilation fold out near the top. Some tepees took several efforts by us volunteers to perfect this construction. Workers hoped for preciseness.

Peace researcher Vaclav Havel says *hope* means that something makes sense *regardless how it turns out*. Margaret Wheatley, writer and organizer, says Havel is actually describing hopelessness, which is not a bad thing. She recalls Buddhist teachings saying hopelessness is "not the opposite of hope. Fear is. Hopelessness is free of fear and can feel quite liberating. Clarity and energy emerge."

Isn't that what we are trying to do at Holden? We could dialogue about these things, in the sauna or build a sweat lodge. Don't we want both clarity and emerging energy?

Galtung promotes the idea that *Singularism* (only one faith) and the concept of being *Chosen People* leads to "over extensions, exposures and vulnerabilities that in the name of defense of pure faith become violent. High levels of self-righteousness lead to concepts of a Holy and Just War."

Islam has a pilgrimage called *hajj*, for stoning the devil. Millions of believers crowd densely in a labyrinth-like setting so tight that about

250 of the pilgrims die at every *hajj* observance, trampled to death at the shrine. Other fundamentalist sects foster killing of family members who disagree with church-sanctioned acts, such as polygamy.

Back in our class with Mary, we students considered questions: What makes people flock toward faith-based physical violence? Do they crave a blood atonement? Where is the line between religious fanaticism and insanity?

"Some religions motivate people toward cruelty," Mary said. "The substitution theme – Christ dying for human sins –influences women especially. They live out the *sacrifice play.*"

An example is in the Virginia Woolf story, *Angel of the House*, where the woman takes the blame, saves the day, rescues others and loses herself. These angel-like women try to be ready, even to be crucified, to show their gratitude to husbands and society. Clearing violence out of the liturgy, as well as our lives, sounded good to me, and a winning dissertation for Mary. I liked the blades of grass symbol, and accepted shit, piss and so on. But not blood and guts.

I wanted to talk about birth, death, and whatever people had on their minds – in that sauna in my head. Some historians claim there will always be Holy Wars like the Crusades that roared through the land in the 11th to 13th centuries. Thoughts about the Reformation raced through my head and showed me hair shirts, beds of nails and examples of extreme fasting. And what about snake handlers, holy rollers and whirling dervishes?

In a modern Filipino Lenten tradition, a male church-member substitutes for Christ on the cross. On Good Friday nails are driven through the man's hands and feet. He and his cross become the lead float in a parade. Medics treat the tortured man's wounds when he is released.

The continued art of rituals, worship, sacrifice of the Mass with consecrated elements, and transfiguration of bread and the wine into Christ's flesh and blood entrenches many people into paying homage to a deity. What did Mary think about that? Where was she leading us? But the last of our one-hour classes galloped to its finish line.

I was once a kid who read sermon titles on local church signs such as "What Heaven Is Like," and I am still curious about religious beliefs. Mary's theological questions will help me continue my search at home or anywhere in the universe.

Although our teacher didn't talk to the class about the forthcoming birth of her child, she must have known that leaving the womb is humanity's introduction to violence. We surge into the world on the tide of breaking water, pushed by muscle contractions, and under delivery-room bright lights. We are born in violence.

But violence did not present itself in the Chumash Indian Women's Long dance (from sunset to sunrise) which I had experienced when I returned home from Holden. The sisters showed concern for sisters, grandmothers and a tradition of peace and a variety of dance steps. But when the sun rose, with exceptional glory, I was ready to go home.

When Violence Trumps Everything

My play
I wear blades of grass
listen to sweet violins
go limp when arrested.

Our deal
begins with tumultuous
exit from womb.

You play the violence card
 with standing army and navy
 call yourself peace-keeping players.

Dummy takes the trick
crime fills prisons
brutality drives art
liturgy worships crucifixion
universe hammers with big bangs.

Who wins the contract
 war moguls
 violent felons
 murderous interrogators
 members of defense department
 munitions profiteers
 elected leaders?

I will play the joker
for all females
who trump violence
with genes tuned
into two-generation
increments of peace
for a liturgy of glee.

My grandchildren it's your turn
with blades of grass
sweet violins
and falling limp
when arrested.

barbara marysdaughter

Part Four: The Return

Chapter Nineteen
The Sobering Wilderness

Like a Russian doll nesting ever smaller dolls inside of it, I house an infinity of selves. Daphne Merkin, American writer

The woman wrote a few words about herself and her plans for a week at Holden: "Coming to the wilderness should be an interesting experience because it will be the first time I have ever been in the wilds sober. (Signed) Helen."

Dianne handed me this paper when I volunteered to greet a member of the Seattle detox-treatment group arriving on the early bus for a week at Holden. We greeters should sit next to "our" person at lunch and vespers, answer questions and try to be helpful. After 28 days in the village, I felt I could do that. Especially since Helen sounded like she had a sense of humor.

I had never been asked to help anyone as a teenager or young adult. I didn't know how to go about it but the idea of being useful appealed to me. In my late twenties I found opportunities with orphans and underprivileged children.

This greeter job might be a bigger challenge. I planned to start with listening to Helen. My contact with her might begin a life-long friendship. We could look at the clothes in the attic, and each wear a crazy red wig. Eating together, we might share stories, and an awareness of nature. The beauty and freshness of the wilderness could be a soothing concept for her. And yes, we would be sober.

The yellow bus from Lake Chelan boat dock lumbered toward us. Expectation hung in the air. About ten villagers, including Dianne, greeted the newcomers with introductions, hugs, and chatter that floated above the group. Joanne, a young volunteer, welcomed a woman in a wheelchair and deftly transferred her to Holden's motorized vehicle for the handicapped. All smiles and efficiency with cart and baggage, Joanne followed along to the ramp at Lodge Three. I wanted to do as well with Helen.

Checking each tag, I searched for Helen. Most of the 15 people who disembarked looked like Native Americans. Dianne called to me: "The name you had, *Helen*, didn't come. I'm so sorry."

Disappointment and relief battled in my heart. Did Helen lose confidence at the last moment? Did I, too? Going in for lunch by myself,

I knew Ted would be at one of the tables. The large main dining room buzzed with talk and laughter. I could find friends among the 200 lunch-munchers, even newcomers from the Seattle project. This woman who didn't come on the bus today might be more alone than I have ever been. Helen would never experience this particular wilderness community, this singular time.

Some say you have to live here "to get it," the specialness of the village. Described by early-day supporter Elmer Witt, Holden resembles "vacant-lot play where we can express ideas and feelings, expand horizons. It's a place to agree to disagree, share, argue, try outlandish visions... in unimaginable ways."

Sometimes we sing at mealtime. What would the Seattle-center woman think if we sang, to the tune of *Silver Bells*: "It's dish-team time in the kitchen...dishes piling; it's reviling..."

Or: "When you're snackin' between meals, And you have food left, wrappings or peels, The dining hall has a compost bin. The food goes there but don't look in."

Would she like the Holden hug, held as long as huggers wanted? Today Norm Habel, former director from Australia, made announcements wearing his purple-satin cape and a milk-carton hat. At any time, the kitchen staff might come out doing a conga line, with most of us getting up to dance with them while the Drum Circle kept the beat.

What would my woman guest have thought about Dave, the Head Waitri, wearing a tuxedo today, with a white towel draped over his left arm? I asked the people at my table, "What's up with Dave?"

"It's his last day," said Rose, across from me. "He's waiting on tables. Look he's bringing some ketchup to those people over there."

Waitri set the tables, provide second helpings, and clean up but they don't wait on tables. Except Dave, today. A handsome man, maybe forty at the most, he had dressed for Founder's Day parade like a woman hippie with a huge flower behind his ear. Now he had became an elegant Maitre d'.

"Dave, Dave!" Our table tried to get his attention. Everyone wanted to give him orders. He dashed around and never noticed our efforts.

"Hold up some money," I suggested.

"Who has any?"

"I've got a dollar," said a young woman at our table, digging in her pocket. She gave the bill to Rose who held it high. Dave roared by in overdrive. The green-stuff caught his eye and he skidded to a halt.

"What can I do for you?" he asked, taking the bill.

"Just ice water. When you have time."

He returned in a moment, bowed, placed the pitcher on the table and returned the dollar. The white towel on his arm remained intact as he took off for another summons. I wished my Seattle-woman could have shared with me this lunch that served good food and jokes.

A young guest requested his Happy Birthday song in the "Beatles' style." Dianne, at the mike looked at a loss as she searched the room for someone to do that. Fun people at the other end of the hall started singing, "Yeah, yeah, yeah," and we all pulled it off.

"It's impossible to be together and not sing," Holden's first director Carroll Hinderlie had said forty years before. "A celebration is to *belong*; you can't be alone."

Was my absent guest alone? Ted caught my eye from a distant table and waved. I felt loved, appreciated and thought of this woman by herself in Seattle. The sun shone here and we laughed and joked with each other. Did Helen know how healthy laughter is? It's an aerobic exercise; laughing out of control stimulates circulation, tones muscles and much more.

"We needed to laugh at the Village so it wouldn't be an idolatry," said Hinderlie, self-described as "God's joke." "We didn't want Holden to be taken too seriously." He favored "playfulness, holy carelessness, going on holidays, rejoicing in celebrations, and serving one another." Like Dave, on his last day of work.

At breakfast the next morning, the day of his leaving, Dave stood at the dining-hall mike and told us serious things. The boisterous dining hall quieted down as he described his previous bouts with depression and suicidal urges. We listened to this fun guy whom we had known with a flower behind his ear, in the tuxedo from the costume attic. Now he wore jeans and shirt.

Dave compared his story to an Exodus account of Miriam, big sister of Moses. "Holden was my Miriam, who had all the answers," he said, "and Lake Chelan became my Red Sea. Those dreaded chariots, horses and riders that chased me, they sank to the bottom of the lake."

In his deepest depression, Dave explained, he couldn't get out of bed. The idea of traveling was insane, he said, although a friend gave him boots and suitcase. That inspired him to take a little trip but it was cut short when he missed connections. He said he bungled that excursion but the airline gave him a Frequent-Flyer bonus that was enough to bring him here.

"Holden did the job," he confided to his audience, "but this was not easy."

How would Helen have related to his story? Was she struggling with depressed feelings, plus cravings for a drink? Was there no one to tell her story to, or to laugh with? Who could lead Helen out of a wilderness of binges and hidden bottles? At least I could have made a connection, even a difference. Maybe she could have listened to my story of harassment, counseled me, given advice. Should I become a Nancy Drew or Miss Marple to solve our mystery?

A friend of mine, whose family had moved to many different desert locations, told me about a contact she had at age three, with a horned toad. "I found this toad living in a trash heap in our yard," Kay said. "She let me touch her warty skin, and her baby. Each time we connected, in this way I felt great trust, wholeness, and a sense of home."

My friend said that in her grown-up life she attended the Native American ceremony called the Long Dance. Joining the women dancers, she reclaimed the feeling she had with the toad: "The same trust, wholeness and sense of home, all connected by a delicate thread."

The thread of Holden brought answers that helped Dave, and Ted and me. Ted's carpentry projects, and quiet chats over coffee with fellow workers gave him creative release and stability. I picked up ideas from classes and human conversation. Helen would miss out on this delicate healing thread of connection.

That evening a Holden speaker's story of forgiveness told her rapt audience about terrorists who had killed this woman's 23-year-old daughter in a South African café. She listed steps she took to reach forgiveness for the three men who had fired the guns.

My heart went out to this brave woman who had done what one ought to do: forgive the unforgivable. She actually did it. The audience reacted with awe and admiration that filled the room like a healing salve. Intrigued by her reasoning, I copied down her main points:

> We had to accept the fact that our Western world's law takes over our revenge.

> This is quite separate from personal forgiving which I did by sending a message to the killers of my daughter. I gave up my justifiable right to revenge.

I accepted any violation of my rights as a devaluation of myself.

To overcome that personal devastation, I celebrated the empathy and acceptance that came to me. It also came to the killers after my forgiveness was accepted by them. They regained their humanity.

As a restorer, I found empathy, acceptance, emotional healing, self-worth and peace. My feelings of injustice, and loss of human rights will remain. But hate, fear, anger and revenge are gone.

What a choice! My throat sticks with any affirmative answer. Which of the two groups – (1) injustice and loss of human rights, or (2) hate-fear-anger-revenge – which of them allow a good life? Can I live with injustice easier than with hate and fear? How can I be hilarious?

Not wanting to be an angry vengeful woman, I might decide to give up some human rights, and definitely bow to this mother of a murdered young daughter, in support of her decision. She has given up many rights and a demand for justice, in exchange for freedom from hate, fear, anger and revenge.

In three years of legal battles, Ted and I still feel cheated and helpless in an unjust system that trampled our human rights. We and the neighbors, all of us, lost our humanity in the process, whether or not we recognize that problem. This mother's ideas, which she said came from Jesus' forgiveness of his murderers, could help all of us in pain: rulers, entire countries, the world, the re-hab guests, and Ted and me.

She explained further that a tense political situation at the time threatened the Union of South Africa. Civil war was a possibility if the courts convicted the defendants. Against that backdrop, she accepted the court's ruling that the killers go free.

The high point for her, she said, arrived as a letter from the murdering terrorists. The young men admitted their guilt and confessed sorrow about the death of her daughter. The three men claimed that the mother's ability to forgive them would never be forgotten. That's the part of this extraordinary story that stops me cold with its points of perfection. Exquisite and brilliant vibes run down my spine and I know she has done the right thing.

Battling nations, or neighbors, can learn from these steps of forgiveness. Our case of harassment lacks the heart-breaking murder of innocent people, which might change our thinking. The idea of a murdered Ted, injured or disabled family members or friends, or any of us slaughtered is horror at a new level. Still I see similarities.

We had been counseled to sue our neighbors to obtain a judge's ruling to stop the harassment. That was when we handed over our revenge to the courts, before we knew the neighbors were sociopaths – without a conscience and adept at lying. Judge, arbitrator, arresting deputy believed the neighbors' false claims. Legal rulings slammed against us.

A peacemaking effort, Livingroom Dialogue caught my attention. Started by Jews and Palestinians in the midst of their continuous bombings, the idea has spread to other countries. Broadening to include diverse religions and political beliefs, the primary principles are "listening to the story of the other person." It continues to work. That means full-time listening; where no one inserts an answer starting with "Yes, but..."

A demonstration on the Cal Poly campus, about 25 miles from our home, attracted me one Sunday along with an audience of 50 students and community members. We listened to amazing stories of Jewish ancestors who had to walk from Russia to Shanghai, and a Palestinian family forced to move from their one-year-old home that had been a lifelong dream.

We in the audience of the demonstration witnessed this understanding mode in its glory when each listener repeats the story teller's tale. Points remembered, impressive details poured forth with nothing left out or suppressed. Each saw the similarities in their lives, customs, even using their hands when they talked. Participants' dialogues came from the heart, deep within, and were received with reverence and gratitude.

The Palestinian man admitted his first reaction to the idea of dialogue: "I'll tell those Jews what they did to my family." But his feelings softened. New information changed him.

"We are beginning to want the best for each other and to cooperate as never before," the leader told us. "This is a big point, missing in most of the peace process. It's something officials can't do; it's up to us citizens."

At the college-campus demonstration, the dialoguers as educated people could express themselves, assimilate what they heard, and see the parallels with their own stories. Yes, it all sounds remarkably hopeful. How could this work with two sociopaths?

"Why don't you move?" friends often ask after hearing our story of irrational, vindictive neighbors and relentless harassment. We have no easy answer. Boards and nails, a metal roof, eight big windows, and shiny wood floors can't be worth the continued suffering we have endured every day. We love our home but it's not just the house.

Our land has two flowing creeks, a living part of creation we nurture. Each oak and bay tree decorating our rolling hills brings us joy just by being there. Glistening stones in the creek beds intrigue our geological yearnings; we examine roundness, stripes and unread messages.

We walk among wildflowers and sit under a favorite oak to look through its branches. A scrub jay squawks at us. A circling turkey vulture listens to our silly chatter each time she dips down to sniff out our deadness or aliveness. This is the place we have loved for forty years, and want to share with family and friends until we are too old. Then, only then, will we move.

My fear of going home from Holden begins to disappear. Calmer, less angry, no longer vengeful, I hope I am not fooling my "infinity of selves." Ted, too, is seventy-seven different people, like the *Maruska*. Some savvy and others naive. I know it sounds strange but I believe we are bonded by our escape into the wilderness.

Aggkaka

(AUTOGRAPHED Aug. 2002; *Excellent! I know it sounds strange but it's great, Meishei M.*)

7 eggs
1/3 C sugar
1 T salt
5 C milk
2 1/2 C white flour

Beat eggs, then add sugar and salt. Stir in half of the milk and the flour. Add remaining milk. Grease and flour a 9 X 13" cake pan and pour in the batter. Bake at 425 degrees for 30-45 minutes or until golden brown. Serve with syrup, lemon juice and powdered sugar.

Chapter Twenty
Leaving On the Early Bus

There is no enemy.
   Gandhi

Our reservations called for the early boat and early morning bus. Ted and I had to finish packing the night before while we balanced on the brink of our good-bye to Holden. But this day, different from any other, started for everyone in the village with fear.

In the early morning, just past midnight, Holden's electric cart for disabled had been found abandoned on the trail past the ball field and labyrinth. Its dead batteries suggested the first sniff of concern and trouble. The next alarm sounded at breakfast time when a man named Daniel, member of the Seattle recovery project, could not be found.

During announcements, Dianne told us that Daniel might have driven that cart till its batteries gave out, and continued on foot into the wilderness. "He was not disabled," Dianne said. "He could be lost now, anywhere in these mountains."

Possibilities of rapacious bears, cougars and seductive steep climbs with no return, confronted the lost man. Thoughts of "my" woman from Seattle, Helen, activated all senses of responsibility I might have. To be someone's greeter in the wilderness meant more than I had thought. I wondered who had been Daniel's "special friend" here at Holden. Questions about the lost man bulked up in my mind, overtaxed my brain.

But village emergency-mode prevailed and there was no time for talking. Villagers formed search teams. Medics assembled water bottles, first-aid kits, and blankets. Shovels and ice axes piled up. Searchers scoured the area near the stranded cart. Holden's radio operator contacted the sheriff in Chelan, whose department often responded to emergency calls from our isolated village.

A winter medical emergency, when an avalanche had caught two villagers out skiing, remained vivid in my memory. One skier with a broken arm and a belief that his friend was dead, walked back to the village. Late afternoon twilight ruled against a helicopter rescue, but the pilot counted on a bright moon to make a safe flight. He found the other skier alive, with a broken neck.

The experienced rescue team flew the injured man out and he survived. Heroic rescues instill hope for such cases as Daniel. Out on the green, many of us watched the sheriff's helicopter circle the village and land on the copper-tailings dump. Well-trained bloodhounds had arrived, along with their handlers. These dogs, who walked through our crowd, seemed eager to work. Their droopy sad eyes, brown and black fur gave them a formal, funeral look. Like the celebrities they were, the dogs ignored us and joined the deputies' search party, along with more Holden men.

With our room already assigned to someone else, Ted and I might have to sleep in our tent if we miss the boat. A kitchen worker had come up to us the day before to ask, "Does your room have a double bed?"

Surprised to see the kitchen worker who helped me get my cookbook autographed, I answered, "No, two single beds."

He turned away. "Too bad."

Now Ted and I were down to one sleeping bag and a tiny tent. How many people were prepared to camp out in emergencies like this? I put my hand on Ted's arm. "Maybe we're not leaving after all."

Holden trucks took rescue teams to staging area at the site of the abandoned electric cart. The village emptied like a wartime town, hinting at battles and death. Young, strong men offered powerful hearts and energy to save this one man from whatever devils he battled. Was Daniel escaping Holden, the Seattle project, or life?

Regular schedules meant nothing on this day at Holden. No one could leave the village without a driver for the old school bus, someone to handle the tricky eleven miles to the lake. Ted and I added our luggage anyway to the loading-dock collection of boxes and suitcases, in the strange quietness of our deserted village.

Gloom hung on all our shoulders like a burden. This wasn't normal, not the way things should be. It was a major blip on our intentional life at Holden. The day was screwed up, confused by a new challenge bearing down on us, boring through our outer shells into gut cavities and soft viscera.

The changed schedule had to be dealt with. We might not make the early fast-boat or afternoon one but could go the next day. Or the following. Could we villagers accommodate these changes? Didn't we see it as necessary during the hunt for a missing man?

All of the village's working trucks waited at the end of the road for operation rescue. Abandoned was the early-morning system of Holden's stake-truck carting luggage to the boat dock ahead of the school bus. Our departure time approached.

At 10:30 the old yellow bus rumbled over the gravel road from its garage with Director Dianne at the wheel. Concerned about us villagers, she always seemed to me one of the angels here. With her compassionate expression of interest, she listened to us and showed competence in solving village problems.

Our director put on leather gloves to manage the steering wheel for the miles of sharp switchbacks, and opened the front door. She studied the huge pile of luggage. One of the departing villagers was Mike, our medic, moving out after a year's stay. He had ten times as much to take out as we did. Dianne came up with a solution: "Let's see if we can pile it all in the bus."

She opened the back emergency door. Strong young women, like Katie the carpenter, and Nicole, our new gardening boss (Jennifer had returned to grad school), lifted boxes and arranged them on the back seats. In spite of all the cargo, we passengers only numbered six: three men, two women and a child. There was room. We helped move things along, and checked the time.

"Will we catch the early boat?"

No one knew. Bus-driver Dianne answered another passenger's question: "No, I haven't driven the bus for awhile, but I have done it before."

With cargo loaded, Ted and I took a seat by the front door. The others sat nearby. Dianne struggled with the stick-shift till it made a grating shriek. "I'll get used to it. Don't worry."

Bang, clang, thud. She closed the front and back doors automatically from the driver's seat. The young "longshore-women," exhausted from handling cargo, sat on the loading dock and waved good-bye.

Ted had worked with Katie, who reminded him of our own resourceful daughters. Nicole had moved in across the hall from us. We met her once at midnight when she was coming home from a party, and we were making trips to the bathroom.

We waved back at the young women, and a few other villagers who gathered to see us off. But there were no drums. The bus crept toward the trees. Ted and I stared ahead, anticipating the sharp turns.

I felt "path oriented" like that 87-year-old activist described by Margaret Wheatley in "Letting Go of Hope." The former Spanish Civil War fighter explained, "I do the work, I walk the path, whether we win or lose." That was us travelers on this day which was like none other.

We all traveled that road now. Vibes from our driver penetrated my senses as she concentrated, prayed, maybe tried a Shi-bashi meditation for the lost villager, while directing the lumbering bus toward the lake.

Dianne planned an October wedding, she had told us. I had not met her prospective bridegroom but knew they had met at the village. She encouraged Ted and me to come back for the fall colors, and her wedding with dancing and singing and hilarity. We wanted to "travel that road" but knew we couldn't do it.

My husband's tense alertness soothed my fear of the steep road, the emergency situation. Ready, capable to help, Ted bloomed again as the shining knight Roxanne had called him. On the radio band, a warning came over the air. A male voice said: "There's another bus parked after the third switchback. It's not in your way." We passengers exchanged glances but the voice assured us all: "You can get by. We just wanted you to know."

At each turn of the road, my stomach muscles tensed. I tried to count the endless hairpin curves. The road was like the hiking trail up to the foot of Spider Glacier. We passed the stranded bus, which Dianne had no problem avoiding. Bringing in searchers, that bus had broken down but the rescuers had made it on foot. Maybe they'd even found the lost man by now. Our driver's competence grew with each turn, along with my confidence. We negotiated more switchbacks. Through the open window, I felt fresh lake breezes on my face. Dense stands of trees lined the road.

A small woods awaited us at home, just down the hill from our house. Almost everyday, our dog and I take that trail, winding through the trees to reach our barn and compost pile, next to my vegetable garden. A ritual for Jack-Tar, he explored scents of nocturnal animals who traveled the path while our dog slept. Twice, from the safety of our barn, Ted and I had seen a mountain lion on that trail.

Our woods represent a close-to-home healing-wilderness to me. Each morning when I take the vegetable scraps down the hill, I feel tuned into the animal path, trees along the way, weeds and wildflowers. Jack wags his tail, with nose to the ground. Canine experts claim that is how dogs sniff out their daily news.

In Roxanne's book about Holden's wildflowers, she had rejoiced in watching fawns crash "through the underbrush, leaping over logs and bounding after each other in wild abandonment." Now I thought of the wild abandonment of the lost man.

"If he's a Native American," I asked Ted, "wouldn't that help him survive?"

"You mean like building a shelter with leaves and branches?"

"Yeah, he would know how to hunt for food, too, and start a cooking fire," I continued. "Go-back-to-his-ancestors kind of life. Maybe that was his idea."

No one seemed to know what the man was seeking: peace, quiet, adventure, a new life. Or death. Did he face a vendetta, like we did? Did he escape into the wilderness for healing? What kind of person was he? Did he have a sense of humor?

If he were Navajo, his family would have celebrated his first laugh with a party for his graduation from the cradle board. If he were Apache, he would know that the Great Spirit wasn't satisfied with the first people on earth until they laughed.

We will arrive home with laughter, tears, and resolve to restore neighbors' humanity, and our own. The legal process we followed for three years had ripped any sense of being human from all parties involved. Can we bring it back when we drop our "justifiable vengeful" feelings?

"The government becomes the avenger," says Blumenfeld in her book Revenge. "Through the process of documents, testimony and cross-examination, due-process strips the revenge out of hostility." But the author admits that "courtroom decisions can be horrible, and that people lie."

The law has been called an ass by Mr. Bumble in Dickens' Oliver Twist and I agree. Justice and civil rights may be human inventions, which I support, but if they stand in the way of peace, I will give them up.

We might see that we have neighbors with a deep hunger, paraphrasing a quote from Frederick Buechner, and we may find a deep gladness in solving the puzzle. If Ted and I need to treat the neighbors as though they were better people than they have been for the past three years, we will find that difficult. To restore our humanity and theirs, too, may be frustrating work. Will it lead to deep gladness?

A poet named Jon Arno Lawson published a book titled *Love Is an Observant Traveler*, illustrated by artist Lui Lui. I started reading the book while visiting Lui in his home in Toronto, Canada, and found an unforgettable quote from Lawson's poem titled *Bad News*:

Humanity does not have a long fuse
and this generation holds the last match

The words had stopped me. Not because I understood what the lines meant but because of its urgency. Whether the last match would blow up humanity (because we are a time bomb), or fuel it for another term, I did not know and I am not sure what humanity is.

Edward O. Wilson's book *Concilience* defines humanity as being akin to all life forms. Recognizing our common descent, we find everything related and are shirt-tail cousins to all of it. Wilson calls science "a continuation on first stories of where we came from." He considers good questions more important than the answers and that may be because they are un-answerable.

Page-turner is a job definition offered by Holden's former spiritual director Marlene Muller. She says she's a helper, a counselor offering assistance. I want someone like her to answer those questions, turn pages while I sing a libretto of suffering, endurance and hope. Most of my efforts have come to nothing; here's part of my first conciliatory letter to our woman neighbor:

I thought I'd communicate with you by note since Saturday's phone calls were unsettling. Neither Ted nor I have ever had this kind of experience before. However, I do believe we have to continue our conversation. In the future, I will do more listening, will not defend myself but will try to understand what is going on. I beg you not to put a lock on the gate for a number of reasons: emergency vehicles, deliveries (FED EX & UPS come right to our door), guests and relatives cannot get through, and the difficulty I have opening locks in the dark.

We received no response. The next stage for me became chanting/singing: *Some day we will walk arm in arm* After weeks of that, came my writing of 100 identical sentences: *There will be peace on our roadway*, and I believed those words for we are all connected, residing in this community of humanity. I tacked the 100 sentences on my bulletin board and waited, afraid to write more letters or make another phone call.

Yet for this after-Holden stage of our struggles, Ted and I agreed on the point of inaction that delivers this message: *We will do no harm.* That should be a given; we shouldn't have to make a point out of it.

Blue waters of Lake Chelan sparkled through the tree tops as we approached that last descent and turned toward the shore. Our *Lady of the Lake* boat, tiny on the great expanse, plowed through water-ripples toward the dock. Ted announced, "We are in time."

The scene looked postcard-perfect, and the air made breathing a delight. Even my tongue tasted its freshness. Our angel-driver braked down the last steep part of the road, put on the emergency and opened the front doors. "You had better get out because I have to back the bus onto the pier."

That long-and-skinny wood-planked pier stood twelve feet above the surface of the lake. Dianne conquered the challenge. We passengers assisted with luggage carried to the boat people. The entire pile of all our belongings disappeared into the ship's hold.

This lake, dock and boat presented the outside world to us. After thirty-three days in the Glacier Peaks Wilderness, I greedily stretched my vision across the narrow lake to all of the world I could see.

"Look how much has been blackened by the brushfire." Ted pointed out.

He's obsessed, I thought, and should have been the fire chief. He understands fire. When threatening fires in August 2004 forced the village to evacuate 450 people, a group of thirteen became "left-behinds" to protect the village. They helped the fire fighters, and prepared to leave only when the words came "Go now." While waiting, they perfected Holden's sprinkling system to work unattended and indefinitely, to protect the wooden buildings. Ted could have worked on such a project.

I examined our excursion boat, 100 ft. long with two decks. Lots of passengers who had boarded at Stehekin leaned on the railing and traded stares with us. Could they tell that we had been cloistered in the woods?

This was our coming out party. Ted and I had been hermits from society, living out volunteer-simplicity concepts, within sustainable ecology, getting along with less, without electronic gadgets. Like a newborn marveling at everything, I found this re-entry world intriguing, different from the one we had left, and offering us infinite possibilities. I wanted to dance into this world, learn to play the cello and sing, bellowing like I'm having a calf.

Our five-hour boat ride started the journey home. We stood on the deck in the stern of the boat to wave to Dianne, to the pier, to the bus. I searched for the Holden road, beyond the trees, and for favorite mountain peaks, but nothing looked familiar from this angle. The world was fresh and new; all muddiness had been swept out and there were no rules.

Ted found folding chairs for us and the boat made wakes in the water to send us onward and to mesmerize our minds. Clouds echoed the shapes of the waves. Everything blended. My husband indicated more burned areas on the far side.

The boat's engine droned, mixed fumes with wilderness air. A great weariness forced both of us into a stupor. Incapable to do anything else, I looked at the naturalness of steep banks growing into rocky spires where century-old pine trees pierced the skyline, and creeks helplessly flowed down into the lake. I remembered that crazy red wig I had meant to wear, but never did, glad I had sung for Sara, and placed that keepsake deer-bark back in the woods.

We were spectators, no longer part of that picture. Still, having been there changed everything. I felt we shouldn't have to worry, ever again.

Bonded by our retreat, Ted and I sat together on this boat moving through a wonderfully deep, pure lake, fed by glaciers. Glad that we could travel home together, I recalled how we had arrived separately. Not only at Holden, but our arrivals at birth, ten months and about 800 miles apart.

Of course, I did worry about things. Words on my mind-screen appeared, scribbled and scrawled in disarray: conniving, plotting, lying, harming, threatening, frightening. We had to look at these actions, and ask why have the neighbors been doing this? What do they want? What fueled their vendetta? Did they covet our land, and yearn for us to disappear?

But we were heading home like carrier pigeons with broken wings walking down the common roadway. Back again. Before we got that close, I needed to edit, polish and hone ideas of in-action toward the neighbors, and share a finished plan with Ted.

My intentions began with humane inattention, described with words like heedlessness, non-observance, obliviousness, unmindfulness, holy carelessness. I scribbled these words on a scrap of paper in my purse.

Purse! I hadn't used my purse for one entire month. Carrying my green canvas, leather-bound bag, with keys on the end of its strap, became a formal sign of homecoming for me. I felt less wild, less free, more hounded by a civilization where doors will be locked.

Consulting in my head, with our children, I heard Judy say, "Ignore the neighbors, treat them as aliens, not human. Never look at them."

Modifying Judy's idea, we could acknowledge the neighbors with kindliness when they let us drive through our easement without obstructions. I might wave if they let me go through the gate ahead of them, or for any civil act on their part, no matter how small and inconsequential.

Our middle child, Nancy, leaned toward legal activities and had contacted the Sheriff. I agreed we needed to call the Sheriff's department when the Gnome throws rocks at our cars, spits at us, or the Witch allows unattended mules in the roadway.

When Matt drives through the easement on his motorcycle, he ignores the neighbors if they come out to look. Matt's young-male presence intimidates the Gnome; bullies, I have read, are cowards. I will quit calling them names and speak of them as our neighbors.

We cannot see the absolute ending of the conflict. Ted or I could still be accused of anything – theft, assault, murder. I could be arrested, hauled off in handcuffs, do time in jail, too. There is no guarantee but Ted and I will began to envision a more peaceful future.

In metered time with our boat's motor, my engine of *unperceivement* and *humane inattention* came to life. The neighbors could not be happy people. To see things through their eyes, to think through their minds, might show us the devils they deal with each day, and help us recognize their burden. At the same time, this new knowledge confirmed for us that rational mediation would never work.

Clinging to Gandhi's belief that *there is no enemy*, I chanted a new mantra. Silently in my head, I addressed our neighbors, "I will not impose words or glances upon you because your life is separate from ours. You are free spirits. You can ignore us, too." I wanted to add: *Please, please, please, ignore us.*

As soon as the boat docked, the crew piled our luggage on the pier. Chastened by the weight of my long-held anvil, now weighing 100 pounds, I yearned to throw it into the Red Sea. Dave (Head Waitri) had called this lake by that biblical name. Our anvil now sank with Dave's chariots, horses and riders and all that spectacle. Everything dropped to the deeps at 1500 feet.

Easily strapping my light backpack onto my shoulders again, I adjusted my purse's strap and picked up my duffel. Life looked easier. Ted carried two duffels and we walked to the parking lot where our car had waited for a month.

Ted's eyebrows met in a dark frown. He touched the hood of our van. The brushfire across the lake had layered fine ashes all over the burgundy paint job.

"It doesn't matter," I said, though I understood how he grieved over the vehicle.

His hands examined the top surfaces, then the doors. "It'll never come off."

The ashes on our car had to be removed, the lost man needed to be found, and harassment must be washed out of our lives. My eyes brimmed with tears, at the welcome-home work still to be done. I climbed into the car as my brain flooded with a hapless clutter of cleaning house, weeding gardens, attacking overgrown poison oak and new paths. Ted started the engine and spit out the healing words: "I'll look for a car wash in Chelan."

That's when I knew there was no enemy and no problem without an answer.

Untoward Afterword

Back Matter is another name for what this is: an attempt to answer readers' questions. Some potential readers may look at this first, and that's OK, too.

What has been important to me is sharing with readers our family's journey (spiritual and literal) following the wrongful arrest of Ted, husband of 50 years, father of three, outdoors-man, engineer and physicist, and more. Our shared life came into focus at Holden Village Ecumenical Retreat Center, in Glacier Peaks Wilderness, Washington state.

Surprises, perversity perhaps, and more than six senses of humor pulled us along the healing path. The power of laughter may seem like nothing but air, thin or thick. However, breath escapes from our lungs in laughter, with snorts, explosive gasps, giggles and guffaws; hilarity becomes a blessing from the earth, to the universe.

A young friend of ours said she married her husband because he made her laugh. I was drawn to Ted because he chuckled at my jokes. Two bereaved Seniors discovered they both subscribed to the *Funny Times* and, with confidence, set their wedding date.

The first director of Holden Village, Carroll Hinderlie, said he and fellow prisoners of World Was II reacted with laughter when released. With that experience, Hinderlie named Holden Village's first summer theme: Holy Hilarity. Writer Lorri Moore filled two facing pages with 70 lines each, with the words Ha, Ha, Ha. The woman in Moore's story laughed at her husband's unfaithfulness, in order to salvage her own life.

Laughter is a universal gift holding us in caring concern. Ted and I, on this Golden Wedding trip, broke out of our jail of fear to laugh, become care-less, to consider howling like wolves, to salvage our lives.

We hope to hear from readers who unhappily suffer from sociopath neighbors, or co-workers. I don't wish that upon my readers but realize that could be the reason they were drawn to this book. In the past year, we have heard from eight people in our area who experienced similar harassment, and one woman on the east coast. They responded to a book review I wrote in a local paper.

One out of 25 people is a sociopath, according to some clinical surveys. (Others say one out of fifty.) There are many (perhaps 5000) in our San Luis Obispo county. Working together, a group with similar experiences may be able to find solutions. Ted and I keep our lives as calm as we can. You may contact us at the email address below and we will try to help and/or put you in touch with others for group solutions.

For those reading these words after finishing the book, you will want to know that after returning home, our encounters with the troublesome neighbors continued, but in a more relaxed way. We still receive curses, obstructions appear on the roadway, deputies are summoned, but no arrests have occurred. We have survived with no hiring of lawyers, and no legal confrontations since the Holden retreat.

But that man lost in the Glacier Peaks Wilderness on our departure day, he has never been found.

Peace like a glacier, Barbara Mary Johnson

redbarn@calinet.com

Bibliography

Balanced and Restorative justice project: www/barjproject.org

Brown, Rosellen, *Before and After*, Harper Collins, Canada Ltd., 1992

Bryson, Bill, *Walk in the Woods*, Broadway Books, NY

Bunyan, John, *Pilgrim's Progress*, Element Books Ltd., 1997

Cameron, Marion, *Karma & Happiness*, Fairview Press (Center for Spirituality and Healing) 2001

De Assisi, Machado, *Don Casmurro*, Oxford U. Press, NY 1997

Duncan, David James, *My Story as told by Water*, San Francisco, Sierra Club Books, 2001

Grimstad, Roxanne, *Wildflowers of Holden*, Holden Village Press, Chelan, WA 1998

Holden Village News, Spring 2001, Vol. 39, HCOO-Stop 2, Chelan, WA 98816-9769

Holden Hi-Lights, Spring 2002, Vol. 42, HCOO-Stop 2, Chelan, WA 98816-9769

Hutchinson, Katie, *Walking after Midnight: One Woman's Journey through Murder, Justice and Forgiveness*, New Harbinger Publications, Inc. Oakland, CA

Killion, Tom and Snyder, Gary, *High Sierra*

Lal, Lakshmi, *Myth and Me: The Indian Story*, Rupa & Co., New Delhi, India 2003

Lutz, Charles P., *Surprising Gift: the Story of Holden Village Church Renewal Center*, Holden Village Press, Chelan, WA 1987

McPhee, John, *Encounters with the Archdruid*, Farrar, Strauss, Giraux, NY 1971

Merriam, Karen, *Searching for Connection*, Truthsayer Publishing, San Luis Obispo, CA, 2006

Mitchell, John Hanson, *Following the Sun: A Bicycle Pilgrimage from Andalusia to the Hebrides*, Counterpoint, WDC, 2002 (Johnson reviewed book: Nimble Spirit *webpage*)

Newberg, Andrew, et al: *Why God Won't Go Away: Brain Science & the Biology of Belief*, Ballantine, NY 2001

Nisker, Wes., *A Practical Guide to Discovering Your Place in the Cosmos: Budha's Nature*, Bantam, NY 1998

Raffa, Jean Benedict, *Dream Theatres of the Soul: Empowering the Feminine through Jungian Dream Work*, Innisfree Press, Inc., Philadelphia, PA 1994

Stout, Martha, *The Sociopath Next Door, the Ruthless Versus the Rest of Us*, Broadway Books, NY, 2005

The Forgiveness Project: www.theforgivenessproject.com

Williams, Terry Tempest, *Refuge*, Vintage Books, NY, 1992

Tudge, Colin, *The Tree, a Natural History of What Trees Are, How they Live, and Why they Matter*, Crown Publishers, NY 2005

TAPES:

HiC: *Having Fun with Luther*

75-7: Carroll Hinderlie

HiC: *Life as Festivity*

76-10: Carroll Hinderlie

HiC: *The Happy Exchange*

75-38: Carroll Hinderlie

About the Author

Barbara Mary Johnson is a writer of books and a published play for children. She taught Journalism at the university level, and has been an editor of publications in the printing profession, financial holding companies, and a relief agency. For the latter job she traveled with their film crew around the world to interview refugees in Portugal, Pakistan, Uganda, Somalia, Thailand and the Philippines. Johnson worked as copy editor (polisher) for one year in Beijing's Xianhua News Agency. She holds a Ph.D. in Creative Writing and Literature, a Masters degree in Communication Arts, and a Bachelors degree in Business Administration.

Barbara Johnson has written books on ethics, saying *yes* to change, and maintaining integrity in a dishonest world. Two of her books are bicycle adventures when she and her husband Ted (in their fifties) cycled across the United States. Ten years later they biked from New Orleans to the source of the Mississippi River, carrying a tent and their own gear (no pun intended).

In 1996 Barbara began writing poetry under a new name: barbara marysdaughter. That summer she walked the entire coast of California with four other hikers to claim public access onto beaches and bluffs. In *A Spirited Escape*, she climbs a glacier with her children and grandchildren to find her way to conquer problems at home with neighbors, and a shared universe.

Printed in the United States
94033LV00003B/68/A